EATING AT HOME COOKBOOK

A Paperback Original
First published 1990 by
Poolbeg Press Ltd.,
Knocksedan House,
Swords, Co. Dublin, Ireland.

ISBN 1 85371 096 2

Cover design by Pomphrey Associates
Typeset by Typeform Ltd.
Printed by The Guernsey Press Ltd.,
Vale, Guernsey, Channel Islands.

Biddy White Lennon's

EATING AT HOME COOKBOOK

POOLBEG

Contents

Weights, Measures and Oven Temperatures

Solid Weight Conversions

Imperial	Metric
½oz	15g
1oz	30g
2oz	60g
3oz	90g
4oz (¼lb)	120g
5oz	150g
6oz	180g
8oz (½lb)	240g
12oz (¾lb)	360g
1lb (16oz)	480g

Standards

1oz = 30g 1lb = 16oz (480g)

1g = 0.35oz 1kg = 2.2 lb

Oven Temperature Conversions

°F	Gas	°C
225	¼	110
250	½	120
275	1	140
300	2	150
325	3	160
350	4	175
375	5	190
400	6	200
425	7	220
450	8	230
475	9	240
500	10	260

Liquid Conversions

Imperial	Metric	US Cups
½ floz	15 ml	1 tbsp
1 floz	30 ml	⅛ cup
2 floz	60 ml	¼ cup
3 floz	90 ml	⅜ cup
4 floz	125 ml	½ cup
5 floz (¼ pint)	150 ml	⅔ cup
6 floz	175 ml	¾ cup
8 floz	250 ml	1 cup (½ pint)
10 floz (½ pint)	300 ml	1¼ cups
12 floz	375 ml	1½ cups
16 floz	500 ml	2 cups (1 pint)
1 pt (20 floz)	600 ml	2½ cups
1½ pints	900 ml	3¾ cups
1¾ pints	1 litre	1 qt (4 cups)
2 pints (1 qt)	1¼ litres	1¼ quarts
2½ pints	1½ litres	3 US pints
3¼ pints	2 litres	2 quarts

Length Conversions

1 cm = 0.3 in

1 in = 2.5 cm

Recipe Notes

All cup measurements are American cups (8 floz)

Spoon measurements used for small quantities of solid ingredients mean gently rounded measures

Introduction

Long, long ago, in the days of my hard-working youth, I remember reading a series of American self-improvement books—you know the sort of thing—"Thirty seconds a day with this book will change your whole life in thirty days." None of them really made much difference to me but one of them, I remember, was a time management system for every second of your life. It was so earnest it was laughable—expounding the idea that time and motion management theories should be applied to your personal ration of time, thus making more time available for the things that really mattered in your life.

My "personal time ration" was at that period divided between two full-time jobs, one in television and another in the theatre at night, a small demanding child who required love, nourishment and rearing, plus a husband, for good measure. Though, to be fair to the latter, he tended to save me time rather than spend my time.

I never did master time management. The child has almost reared himself and, while we have a good relationship, his need for mother-love has been diminishing for some time now, in direct inverse ratio to his increasing interest in "other women."

His need for food I finally solved by writing a book for him. *The Leaving Home Cookbook* introduced him to the joys of cooking for himself.

One habit I did pick up from the book about personal time management was to spend thirty seconds every day "thinking-about-myself-and-my-life-style." (Thirty seconds is about all the time I have to spare.) This session is usually spent bemoaning my fate. However, in an early session I did decide that one of the ways I was going to use all this time I was going to save was eating good food.

It has taken me a goodly number of years to perfect the balancing act between slaving unnecessarily in the kitchen and spending money unnecessarily in restaurants. (Processed, ready-cooked food was **never** on the agenda.) I like good food too much ever to fall prey to the ad-man's fantasy that convenience food is the answer. It may well be necessary on the very odd occasion but it has never counted as real food, then or now.

The Eating at Home Cookbook sets out to share with you what has taken me half a lifetime to learn—that it is possible to work long hours every day and still eat good **real** food at home.

The book assumes that you have acquired basic cooking skills. If you have not—be honest with yourself—do not start at the first page of this book; start instead with *The Leaving Home Cookbook*. That book aims to teach the basic skills and provides recipes for **one** person. Once you have mastered the basics, this book will take you the next step down the road.

I have never really accepted the statistical **average** family of four people on which most cookery books are based. It's my experience that you start single, acquire a partner, then need to entertain friends and relatives, before you settle down to produce a family of your own. All the recipes in *The Eating at Home Cookbook* are calculated on the basis of ingredients for **two** people and for **six** people. This is because I believe that you will be cooking for yourself and your partner, your flatmate, your husband, your wife, aunt, or granny most of the time; and that occasionally you will wish to entertain others:

friends, relatives, or business acquaintances. Using this book you can gain confidence cooking the real food recipes for two before scaling them up when you entertain more people.

Real food is a habit which you must acquire. Even in the best-ordered lives, there are days when **time** is the one thing you do not have. Those days are often the ones when you arrive home ravenous. It is at those times that real food resolutions tend to go out the window. With this in mind there is a substantial section of this book which deals with recipes which can be prepared, sometimes with a little planning ahead, in fifteen minutes or less. The recipes are not only quick, easy to prepare, and delicious; they are also nutritionally balanced and often use the sort of ready-to-eat ingredients which **are** worth buying.

I'm a great believer in good bread as an everyday dietary essential. I have devoted a whole section to home bread-making because I have found that it is virtually impossible to buy good bread any more. It is also very easy to make at home and can transform any meal, from the simplest late supper to the most elaborate dinner party.

The section on entertaining contains carefully chosen recipes which can be prepared ahead of time so that you are in a position (and a fit state) to look after your guests and enjoy your own party. The strategy of giving ingredients for two servings and for six allows you to try out these recipes before having to prepare them for guests.

One of the great temptations which takes people into restaurants is the desire to eat food which they feel is beyond their culinary skills, or food that they sampled while on holiday abroad or on a business trip. But it is not necessary to go to a restaurant for these things. Many are simple to prepare at home.

If the book seems to contain a high proportion of recipes which might be loosely classified as Italian, or

Mediterranean, this is because Italy is where I like to spend my holidays. I also find that the Italians have an attitude to food which is very like my own. They like it real, as fresh as possible, and simple. They love contrasting textures and really good bread. Many Italian dishes are startlingly simple to prepare and quick to cook. The Italian diet is also a very healthy one. Olive oil is one of the oils, like fish oils, which can be actually good for you. They also make wonderful use of fruit, vegetables, salads and beans, which are essential if you are to eat a nutritionally balanced diet. Italian food is also economical, useful for those times when money, as well as time, might be in short supply.

Finally, *The Eating at Home Cookbook* sets out to give you a brief introduction to herbs and spices, an essential part of any good cook's armoury. The imaginative and discriminating use of herbs and spices can transform a meal as much as the careful choice of kitchen equipment can simplify its preparation.

1
Equipment

A serious cook needs good equipment. Well-chosen equipment can quarter the preparation-time and make cooking a pleasure rather than a trial.

Small kitchen appliances, as the manufacturers call them, must be carefully chosen and well designed if they are not to spend their lives lurking at the back of drawers and cupboards or, worse still, cluttering the work surface. A kitchen appliance, however small, must pay its way. What is essential equipment for one person can be another person's dust-collection unit. How do you decide what you need?

Never go to Ideal Home exhibitions and do not watch television advertisements. The list of manufacturers' appliances-of-the-year is endless—remember those electric toasted sandwich makers and electric barbecues? One year everyone's persuading you to buy an electric pasta maker, the next they all say you're not living unless you are the proud owner of the latest bread maker which seems to make bread, according to the advertisements, out of silicon chips! Or was that the deep-fat fryer?

I was gullible. I have a dump room in our house to prove it. But I use my silly cone maker, I hear you cry. Just wait until it breaks down and see how long it takes you to get round to driving all the way to that enormous industrial estate at the perimeter of the known world to get it fixed. Talk to someone like me who has been seduced by advertising—every street or apartment block has one.

Then talk to yourself. Seriously! Examine your likes and dislikes. Review your life-style. If you hate pasta, don't buy a pasta maker. On the other hand, if you adore pasta, as I do, then you will use it three or four times a week and gain a reputation for being brilliant at Italian food! Similarly, a toaster is the fastest way of making toast—if you like sliced pan. My toaster broke down five years ago and was discovered recently in the boot of the car when I got a puncture late at night. It had never been missed.

Look at your kitchen and be realistic about what it can fit without requiring major rearrangement whenever you need to use a piece of equipment and without reducing work-space. If your kitchen is small, and because, in my experience, architects never spend any time in their own kitchens they are always smaller than they need to be, then it makes sense to buy neat, multi-purpose units—a food processor with a wide range of attachments, or an electric Dutch-oven which can double as a frying-pan or a slow-cooker. Make a list of essential items and buy them, gradually, from a reputable dealer. A fly-by-night might be cheaper but what happens when the appliance breaks down during the period of guarantee and he's upped anchor and away? Chances are it was a grey-import and not covered by the manufacturer's guarantee anyway! Local service arrangements are vital. You do not want to post a bulky appliance to Scotland, Italy, or South Korea. Check this out before you buy. Experience has taught me to buy from established local suppliers, whose premises have customer car-parking facilities, who are able and willing to service appliances made by established manufacturers. Recently my dishwasher, which has served me faithfully for sixteen years, needed a plastic part replaced. The local supplier was able to get the Italian manufacturer to make the part for me even though the machine has been obsolete for eight years.

Food Processor

I would not be without one. I use mine three or four times a day, every day. A recipe which you would never make because of the time and effort involved becomes the work of minutes rather than hours. You will use it to purée soups, sauces and baby foods; to chop, slice or grate vegetables and fruits, grind meat, knead bread, mix batters, cakes, puddings and ice-cream. It is the modern equivalent of the Victorian tweeny-maid. Buy the most substantial heavy-duty model with the widest range of extras that you can afford.

Combined Dutch-oven/Electric Frying-pan

This is the most wonderful, multi-purpose machine and very few people consider buying it. A great space and money saver which can act as a slow-cooker, a small oven, a controlled temperature frying-pan, a bread prover and dish-warmer.

Deep-fat Fryer

An electric, thermostatically controlled unit, with a heavy hinged lid, good filtration, and comprehensive temperature control is the only safe way to deep-fry foods. Go for a rectangular unit rather than a circular-shaped one and make sure it comes apart easily for cleaning. Buy a good-sized unit. The smaller ones may save on oil if you are just cooking French fries for one or two people but are rarely big enough to cook fish, chicken or other bulky foods without it becoming a major planning operation.

Coffee/Spice Grinder
If you like real coffee you will need this to grind your beans in your own preferred mix. Buy an extra bowl so that the appliance can double as a spice grinder. Spices should always be bought whole and ground as needed to prevent them becoming stale and losing their flavour and aroma. Some units have an optional blender attachment which can be useful to purée soups and baby foods, but this is rarely strong enough to cope with grinding meat or chopping vegetables. It cannot be considered a substitute for a good food processor.

Citrus Juice Extractor
This is an inexpensive but very useful item. One of the few jobs which food processors cannot do successfully is extracting the juice from lemons, limes and oranges without grinding up the pith and pips as well. This makes the juice bitter. A small juice extractor produces large quantities of juice in seconds, strains out the pips and the membranes, and never even gets near the pith. I don't know how I ever did without one.

Electric Knife Sharpener
Blunt knives are dangerous. They slip and cut the cook. For years, blunt knives were a bone of contention in our kitchen, eliciting oaths and much sighing on the part of my husband, one of whose tasks was considered to be the maintenance of knives. Two Christmases ago he appeared with a combined electric tin-opener and knife sharpener. I haven't cut myself since and kitchen quarrels have been halved. (Blunt knives are not the only things two cooks can spoil!) This well-designed unit does away with the need for old-fashioned steel sharpeners which were never very successful with the modern stainless steel blades in any case. It has also relegated the electric carving knife to

the dump room. It was never heavily used but I admit that if you lack strength in your cutting arm, there is a case to be made for using it to prepare evenly sliced bread for sandwiches.

Electric Food Mixer

The kitchen-chef was *de rigueur* in the days before the food processor. Many of these units come with a battery of add-on attachments, but, unless you are heavily into baking, the food processor has banished the large multi-purpose units from most modern kitchens. A small, inexpensive model or, better still, one of the cordless, hand-held units still has a place for whisking egg whites, mixing sponges and whipping cream.

Meat Grinder/Mincer

We use a heavy-duty, manual model for mincing meat, especially for home-made sausages and terrines. The texture of hand-ground meat is better than the pounded pastes that food processors produce. But the food processor is much quicker and far easier to clean.

Electric Pasta Maker

If you like fresh pasta these machines are useful. They produce excellent pasta, in a limited variety of shapes, in about three minutes, as opposed to the hours it takes by hand.

Ice-cream Maker

There is no doubt that these machines make ice-cream with little trouble and their owners swear by them. I can get by, improvising with the food processor and the deep-freeze. Dedicated ice-cream eaters might find that this unit pays its way.

Toasted Sandwich Maker
We had one. I don't know where it is.

Electric Waffle-iron
We had one of these, too. It's probably wherever the toasted sandwich maker is. Maybe if you are married to a homesick American you could justify this item.

Electric/Gas Barbecue
We barbecue food a great deal—because we like the flavour. It's the real charcoal that gives the flavour. Only buy one of these if you like gas-flavoured food.

Weighing Scales
No serious cook can work without accurate scales. Buy the best you can afford. The digital units are very accurate and should be capable of switching between different units of measurement.

Mouli-sieve
There are foods which cannot be successfully puréed in a food processor. Fruits like blackberries and raspberries become bitter in a processor because the seeds get ground up with the flesh. Potatoes become glutinous. Tomato skin and seeds add a taste which is not altogether wholesome. This inexpensive item is essential for these tasks. Buy a sturdy, non-flexible, plastic unit with three different-sized discs.

Thermometer for Fridges and Freezers
Few domestic fridges or freezers have dials which show you the actual internal temperature of the appliance. Until they do, and the signs are that manufacturers may soon be forced by legislation to incorporate them because of growing concern about the correct storage of foods, use one of these inexpensive items and check it daily.

Oven Thermometer

An oven thermometer to check the exact temperature of your oven is essential for bread, cakes and biscuits. I find that some electric oven temperature settings can often be inaccurate and it is my experience that gas oven temperatures can vary from hour to hour. Electric ovens with fan assistance and gas ovens with gyro-flow will have temperatures which do not vary according to the shelf position you are using. This variation can be very useful when you wish to cook foods at different temperatures. But many dishes require precise temperatures and a thermometer is useful to check the temperatures in your oven at different settings, different times of the day, at different shelf placements and different positions on the shelves (back, front, sides). Then you can be confident.

Meat Thermometer

There are two types of meat thermometer. You insert the first type into the thickest part of the meat and leave it there while the meat is cooking until it reaches the desired temperature. The meat should then be cooked. The second type, the so-called instant-read thermometer, is inserted into the food (which can be liquid or solid) when you think it should be nearly done. After 2½ minutes (some instant) it will give an accurate reading of the internal temperature. Both types take the guesswork out of cooking meat.

Sweet Thermometer

You hook these onto the side of the pot when making jams, jellies and sweets. A probe senses the temperature of the liquid in the pot. It can be difficult to get the pot to match the length of the probe.

Hydrometer

Used for measuring the strength of pickles, brines and sugar syrups and in beer and wine making.

Mortar and Pestle

If your coffee grinder doesn't support a second container then you will need a good mortar and pestle for grinding spices. I find the large Italian marble ones particularly good for dry grinding. I use a wooden one for what I call wet grinding, usually the making of pastes involving crushed and pounded garlic.

Microwave Oven

These units have been getting a bad press recently, not altogether fairly. While some units and their manufacturers might be less than blameless, most of the problems are caused by owners not following instructions both for the machines and for the foods they prepare in them.

Used sensibly, they can be a great help to the cook. They are not suitable for all foods and for certain cooking methods. They will never replace a conventional cooker unless you are prepared to live exclusively on precooked and processed foods. No one with any sense wants to do that. Simple microwave ovens cannot roast or bake successfully, even with the use of browning dishes and browning powders during cooking. The so-called combination cookers are exactly that: they microwave the food and use conventional heating elements to produce the browned, crisp effect during microwave cooking. A microwave cooker cannot grill or sauté foods and egg dishes are difficult because the proteins set too quickly.

Fish cooks well in a microwave and most vegetables cook beautifully and quickly. Stews and casserole using high-quality, tender cuts of veal, chicken and pork will work and stocks, soups, pulses and steamed puddings will cook much more quickly. A microwave is good for small jobs like melting chocolate, softening fats, drying breadcrumbs, making porridge as well as, of course, thawing food and reheating food. In many tasks microwaves do save on energy costs and time. Buy a combination unit if you can afford it. A microwave oven should have a maximum power supply of at least 750 watts, three power settings, and a revolving turntable to cut down on the number of times you must switch it off and open it to move the food around to ensure even cooking. Digital timers are much more accurate than mechanical dial timers. You must always observe the standing-time instructions stated in the recipes and cooking instructions. The next chapter explores more fully how you can use a microwave to help you in the kitchen.

Refrigeration

When we had a half-acre kitchen garden, and buying a side of beef and cutting it up for deep-freezing seemed a desirable activity, we bought a huge 18-cubic-foot unit. It broke down after five years and we replaced it with an 8-cubic-foot unit. We have found this more than adequate ever since and this size unit should serve the needs of a family of four adequately.

If you find it convenient to shop only once a week, it is very difficult to do without some form of deep-freeze. You need it to store staples like bread, meat, some vegetables, batch-cooked soups, stocks, casseroles and cakes. If you intend to use it to store only precooked, ready-prepared convenience foods and live near a shop, then I'd be inclined to save my money and let the shopkeeper pay the cost of running the freezer.

Dishwasher

I could not live without it. It keeps the kitchen tidy and cleans dishes far more hygienically than I could. The only extra work it creates is making sure that everything you buy is dishwasher-proof.

CUTTING IMPLEMENTS

Good knives and cutting tools are essential. Buy the very best you can afford and look after them. Buy one or two really good ones in preference to a cheaper complete set of inferior design. Look for solid construction—the top of the blade, called the tang, should run up inside the handle and be attached by metal rivets; there should be a heel at the wide end of the blade to prevent your fingers slipping onto the blade; the knife should be well balanced and comfortable in the hand. Carbon-steel knives are the easiest to sharpen but will discolour and rust if not kept carefully. Stainless steel knives look well but are difficult for the amateur to sharpen without an electric grinder. The most expensive, and best, are high-carbon stainless steel. All knives should be kept in a special rack, not thrown in with the rest of the cutlery. Never put them into your dishwasher. A wooden chopping board is kindest to blades but is an open invitation to germs and microbes unless you are prepared to keep it spotless and regularly scoured.

Chef's Knife

These come in several sizes from 15-30 cm, with wide, heavy blades and are used for chopping vegetables, herbs and all kinds of foodstuffs.

Paring Knife

A small, thin, straight-bladed knife from 7-10 cm; used for peeling fruit and vegetables.

Carving Knife
Long, slender-bladed knife for carving meat.

Boning Knife
A fine point and a large heel. About 15 cm long.

Filleting Knife
This has a pointed, flexible blade and is used for boning and filleting fish and slicing fruits and vegetables.

Serrated Blade
Needed to slice bread, cakes and pastry without breaking up the crumb. You cannot sharpen these at home but they retain their edge for a long time if cared for.

Chinese Cleaver
This is a good multi-purpose tool used by Chinese cooks for almost every trimming and cutting job. The true Chinese cleavers have much finer blades than the heavy cleavers used by butchers. I find one invaluable in place of the quaintly named cutlet bat, for flattening meat escallops.

Grapefruit Knife
This has an upturned blade which is serrated on both edges and is essential for preparing grapefruits and for hollowing out other fruits.

Poultry Shears / Kitchen Scissors
Essential for cutting poultry carcases into pieces without dangerously splintering bones. Don't use it for pruning the roses.

Oyster Knife
Essential if you are addicted to oysters and wish to avoid bloody knuckles and foul tempers. A short, stiff, rather

stubby blade and a heavy knuckle guard are specially designed for the job.

Graters

There are always jobs that it is not worth dirtying the food processor for and the odd job, like grating hard cheese, which is better done by hand. Look out for a four-sided stainless steel model. Ordinary tin ones work well but rust rapidly. Plastic ones are never sharp enough.

Uncle Tom Cobbley and All

There are a hundred and one other purpose-made cutters, graters, corers, olive pitters, fish de-scalers, melon ballers, zesters, and slicers. You will end up with quite a collection of them if you set out to acquire them. I find that a really good, sharp paring knife can replace almost all of them.

2
Using Your Microwave Oven

A microwave oven can seem like an albatross around a cook's neck—unused, unloved and a constant reminder of how easy it is to be seduced by advertising. There is a kind of inverse rule attached to microwaves: the more time you spend cooking, the less likely you are to use a microwave.

This comes about because, while it is very easy to heat up ready-prepared, cook-chill meals in a microwave (after all, complete instructions are printed on the pack), it is far more troublesome and time-consuming to adapt known, loved recipes for microwave cooking. The task seems so daunting and there is always that sneaking suspicion that most foods have a better taste and texture when cooked by conventional methods.

This is not a book about microwave cooking. Still less is it one which takes well-known dishes and tells you how to cook them in a quarter of the time in a microwave. But in this chapter I will give you some tips and techniques for using your microwave to speed up some of your kitchen tasks. Then the albatross will not weigh quite so heavily around your neck!

How a Microwave Works

The key to understanding how to use your microwave is to understand how it works. Microwaves (comparatively short electro-magnetic waves) penetrate the food to a depth of 4-5 cm and cause the water molecules in the food to vibrate over 2,000 million times a second. This vibration produces heat which cooks the food. The heat generated all round the outer layer of the food is conducted to the centre of the food. This is where the principle of "standing-time" enters the equation. If these carefully calculated times are not observed, then the centre of the foods will not have reached a sufficiently high temperature to kill any bacteria.

Safety

Certain foods are more likely to harbour harmful organisms than others—intensively reared poultry is a well-known example. But any food that may have been stored for a time in conditions which you cannot monitor—cooked foods or frozen foods bought ready-prepared—may have been subjected to conditions, of warmth or even temporary fluctuations of storage temperature, which could allow bacteria to multiply. So, for instance, a roast of pork cooked in a conventional oven is more likely to have reached and maintained a temperature of 85°C (185°F), where conventional wisdom tells us harmful bacteria will have been killed, than one cooked in a microwave. This is an area, in truth, which food scientists are only beginning to get to grips with. Always observe cooking instructions and standing-time instructions to the letter when cooking food in a microwave. All microwave suggestions and techniques given in this book are based on a machine with a high setting of 700 watts.

Uneven Cooking

Recent research in Britain has suggested that some microwave ovens do not cook evenly and this seems to apply even to models with turntables or other devices which are supposed to ensure even cooking. It is safer to assume, however tedious, that you need to stir liquids several times during cooking and to move round solid foods as well.

Metal

Never use anything metal—pottery decorated with metal enamels, aluminium foil, foil-lined containers or cartons, pressed tinfoil plates or containers, metal pots, pans or baking tins—in your microwave. Metal interferes with the waves, causing terrifying arcing which can destroy your machine.

Cooking in a Microwave

It is not really possible successfully to roast, grill or fry food in a microwave, despite the countless books and articles which suggest ways of doing so. They will never brown foods without recourse to browning powders and staining liquids; they will never crisp because you need dry heat to crisp food. Frying is a process which demands that a coagulated sealed surface be formed instantaneously on foods and this is difficult, if not impossible, in a microwave. By the same token, the baking of cakes and biscuits is never totally successful except with specially devised recipes. Nor are microwaves very good at producing the conditions of long, slow simmering required to break down the tougher cuts of meat and this is always more successful in a conventional cooker. So what is left? Most vegetables and fish cook beautifully in a microwave, tender cuts of meat and poultry which do not require long cooking-times, pulses, soups, sauces and stocks can all be successfully prepared. Defrosting and reheating foods is a boon and there are many small jobs like melting chocolate and making a roux which can be done very quickly in a microwave. I would never consider a microwave a necessity but used in conjunction with a conventional cooker for bulk-cooking and freezing of prepared frozen foods it can be a great time-saver. Used correctly a microwave cannot harm you or the food. It is not, however, no matter how much some people might wish it, a steriliser. If a food is contaminated by harmful bacteria, a microwave is no better, and in some ways rather less efficient, than conventional cooking methods at killing them off. This is why it is essential to follow to the letter all cooking and standing-time instructions on the packaging of precooked, processed foods.

Thawing Food from the Freezer
Always use the labelled setting for defrosting food. This is usually the lowest setting on the machine. Many foods can be thawed quickly and successfully in a microwave. It is marginally easier to thaw foods that need cooking or reheating than foods which require no further cooking. Most microwaves come with good instruction manuals (some with cookery books) which give you comprehensive instructions and timings for all these different processes. Follow the instructions carefully.

Microwave Short-cuts
After all the warnings it may seem odd to suggest that a microwave can be used to cut corners but I find that I use my microwave most often to do things which would take much longer by conventional means.

Porridge

Serves 1:

30 g quick-cook oatflakes
175 ml (6 floz) water
pinch of salt

Use a deep bowl because the porridge bubbles and "plooters." Stir the oatflakes and salt into the water and cook for 2 minutes on full (700 watts). Standing-time 2 minutes. Serve with cream and sugar.

Serves 2:

60 g oatflakes
350 ml (10½ floz) water
2 pinches of salt

Cook for 3 minutes (700 watts) with one stir half-way through. Standing-time 2 minutes.

Stocks

Cook in a large glass bowl using the ingredients from standard recipes. Cover the ingredients with warm water and cook for 30 minutes (700 watts) after the water has come to the boil. After 5 minutes, skim away any scum which might have formed on the surface. Standing-time 20 minutes. Allow to cool then strain. If you are using pre-cooked poultry carcases reduce the cooking-time to 20 minutes.

Fish stocks take only 5 minutes cooking at the medium setting once the water has been brought to the boil at the top (700 watt) setting.

Roux-based Sauces

Use a large-size glass or heavy plastic measuring jug and a whisk rather than a spoon.

for white sauce:

30 g butter
1 tbsp plain white flour
300 ml (10 floz) milk

Put the butter into the jug and cook on the high setting for 30-40 seconds until it has melted. Whisk in the flour. Add the milk and whisk it thoroughly. Cook on the highest setting for 3 minutes, stopping to stir the sauce well four or five times during this time. Season and add any other flavourings. Cheese will need a further 30 seconds cooking-time.

Brown roux-based sauces can be approached in much the same manner but, because the best ones require a *mirepoix* of vegetables and a long slow cooking to develop the flavours, I find it easier not to use the microwave.

Apple Sauce

2 large cooking apples (Bramley for preference)
5 tbsp water or cider
1 oz butter
1-2 tbsp sugar (or to taste)

Peel, core and chop up the apples into even-sized pieces. Put them into a bowl with the water or cider. Cook at the highest setting for 3 minutes. Stir three times during this time. Add the butter and sugar and cook for a further minute with one stir.

Pulses

The length of time pulses take to cook, even using conventional cookers, is entirely dependent upon the freshness of the dried bean, pea or gram and on their size. There is no way of knowing how long they will take just by looking at the dried pulse. For this reason always shop for your pulses in a large supermarket or health food shop with a regular turnover. That way you can be sure the pulses will not have been sitting on the shelf for ages.

Where appropriate, soak the beans in cold water

overnight and cook them in the microwave in large glass bowls which allow you to cover them with plenty of water. Use a lid as a cover rather than the usual cling-film. You will need to test them frequently when approaching the end of the cooking-time. Protect your hands when doing this as there will be a lot of steam.

Lentils :	try 20 minutes on the highest setting
Haricot or cannellini :	35 minutes on high
Red kidney beans :	about 45 minutes on high
Chick peas :	1 hour on high

Vegetables

Most root vegetables, especially potatoes, need to be completely submerged in water, or the liquid of a stew or casserole, to be successfully cooked in a microwave. The latter situation is not always easy to achieve. They should always be even in size and need careful watching during cooking. Broccoli and cauliflower must be divided into evenly sized florets. Arrange them on a shallow dish with the stalks pointing out to the edge. Cook for only 3-4 minutes. Where the microwave comes into its own with vegetables is when it is used to blanch vegetables prior to dressing them with a sauce, to stir-frying them in oil or butter, or to freezing them. Unlike the conventional manner of blanching vegetables (immersing them in a lot of boiling water and so, inevitably, leaching out some of the valuable minerals, vitamins and other nutrients into the water), vegetables blanched in the microwave need only 4 tablespoons of water to each pound weight of green vegetable. Root vegetables must still be totally immersed. Do not attempt to blanch more than one pound weight at a time. All blanched vegetables must be cooled in cold water immediately to prevent them continuing to cook in retained heat. Frozen vegetables, whether blanched at home or bought ready processed, need only half the normal cooking-time.

Fish

Some types of fish respond extremely well to microwave cooking. Fillets and whole flat-fish can be placed on a lightly buttered plate, sprinkled with a squeeze of lemon juice and some freshly chopped herbs, covered with cling-film (pierce holes in it) and cooked at high setting (700 watts) for 4 minutes per pound. Standing-time 2 minutes. If you are cooking small whole fish like trout, herring or mackerel the tail tends to cook more quickly than the shoulder. With single fish this is not really a problem. However, if you are cooking two or more whole fish together, then arrange them on the cooking plate so that the tails overlap each other. Because of this difficulty I tend not to cook larger, thicker fish in a microwave.

Meat

Only the tenderest cuts of meat respond really well to microwave cooking. This tempts some microwave cookery books into astonishingly stupid recipes for what amounts to stewed fillet steak. I really am tempted to state categorically that meat only cooks well in some kind of sauce and it is essential to stir the sauce and move the meat around four times during the cooking period to ensure even cooking.

Handy Hints

To soften fat for creaming—10 seconds on high
To melt chocolate—1 to 2 minutes on high with one stir
To dry breadcrumbs for storage—3 to 5 minutes on high
To refresh stale roasted nuts—10 seconds on high on a sheet of kitchen paper
To dry herbs for winter use—2 to 3 minutes spread on kitchen paper
To melt gelatine—place the gelatine with the correct amount of water in a cup and cook for 10 seconds
To help juice citrus fruits—10 seconds on high before squeezing

Two Thoughts

Keep the internal surfaces of your microwave spotlessly clean. Food splashes can divert the microwaves, reduce efficiency and cause uneven cooking. Many books on microwave cooking techniques try to pretend that you can do anything in them. They do the machine a disservice. If your first attempt at cooking in a microwave happens to be a roast fowl or joint or a cake, you will be disappointed and lose confidence in the machine.

3

For Your Information

A Glossary of Cooking Terms and Foods

Baste
To moisten the surfaces of a food, usually meat, during cooking in order to prevent it drying out. This can be achieved with fat, stock, alcohol, fruit juice or water.

Beat
To mix foods by beating vigorously with a wooden spoon, whisk or fork to ensure full mixing of different ingredients and to incorporate air into the mixture.

Béchamel Sauce
Melt 30 g of butter in a saucepan over a low heat. Blend in 30 g plain flour with a wooden spoon and cook slowly, stirring, until the butter and flour froth together for 2 minutes without colouring. Remove this roux from the heat and pour in 400 ml of hot milk at once. Beat vigorously with a whisk to bind the roux and the milk. Return to the heat and stir with the whisk until the sauce comes to the boil. Boil for 1 minute, stirring all the time. Remove from the heat and season to taste.

Blanch
To plunge vegetables (usually green) into boiling water for a short time to cook them partially and to preserve their natural colour. Often used as a preliminary step before braising or stewing them.

Blend
A gentler form of beating (akin to stirring) to mix ingredients.

Boil
To cook at the hottest temperature water can reach in an open pot before turning to steam (100°C, 212°F). It is not an ideal temperature for cooking many foods and is most useful briefly to blanch (see above) and tenderise vegetables and to reduce (see below) stocks, sauces and gravies.

Cheese
A high-protein food made from milk. There are literally hundreds of varieties and your diet should regularly contain some cheese. The recipes in this book occasionally call for the following types: a hard "grana" type like Parmesan or Regato; cheddar type; fresh quark; feta, cottage.

The most useful type for cooking is a hard "grana" type. The finest of these is Parmesan but it is wildly expensive. There are others like the Greek Kefalotyri, other Italian types, and the splendid Irish-made Regato. Never buy these cheeses ready-grated. Buy a piece and grate it as you need it on the fine blade of the grater.

Feta is an eastern Mediterranean cheese originally made from sheep or goats' milk. It is splendid cut into small cubes in salads eaten with pitta breads and olives. It should be stored covered in salted water in the fridge and keeps well this way.

Quark is a fresh cheese and must be eaten within days.

I do not find modern "factory" cheddar is very satisfactory for cooking—under heat the solids tend to separate out from the fat and liquids. Real farm cheddars, properly matured by traditional methods, are much better but tend to be expensive. Buy in small quantities.

Cooking Fats and Oils

Fats and oils are similar substances, the most obvious difference being that at room temperature fats are solid (lard, bacon, mutton, pork, butter) and oils are liquid (olive, sunflower, corn, vegetable, peanut or *arachide*). By and large, fats are derived from meat and milk, oils from vegetables and fish. The former are likely to be classified as *saturated* and the latter as poly or mono *unsaturated.*

Different fats will heat to different temperatures without burning and all have a characteristic taste or flavour. Often the taste of the fat is an essential ingredient in the recipe. This is particularly true in recipes which call for olive oil, or butter, or bacon fats. The French claim that *arachide* oil has no taste but I do not agree. It is widely used as the oil in Chinese stir-frying because it has a very high burning temperature.

Butter has a low burning temperature and this can be raised somewhat by mixing it with olive or vegetable oil. When it is crucial to the flavour, the recipes in this book specify the oil required.

Deglaze

After cooking a meat by pan-frying, the residues which stick to the bottom of the pan are dislodged and incorporated into a tasty gravy by adding a small amount of alcohol, boiling water, fruit juice, stock or cream to the hot pan and stirring rapidly while boiling to reduce the amount of the sauce and thicken it.

Dice
To cut into small even-sized cubes.

Dust
To coat lightly with flour which has been seasoned with salt and pepper or spices.

Fry
To cook in fat or oil at temperatures well above 100°C (212°F), the boiling-point of water. (See **Cooking Fats and Oils,** above.) This process converts surface water and internal water in the food rapidly to steam which tries to escape and so prevents the fat entering the food. The outer proteins coagulate rapidly to form a seal to keep out the fat and keep in the juices and flavour.

Marinade
A mixture of oil, wine or wine vinegar, lemon juice, herbs or spices used to flavour or, more usually, to tenderise meat or fish before cooking.

Mayonnaise
I make my mayonnaise at home in a food processor. I put 2 egg yolks into the bowl with 1 tablespoon of lemon juice and a pinch of dry mustard powder. I process this for 10 seconds and then with the machine working I add 250 ml olive oil (or an equal mixture of olive and vegetable oils) in a steady, thin, continuous stream. It takes about 2 minutes for the mixture to become thick and creamy. I then add the remaining lemon juice, some salt and freshly ground black pepper (to taste) and process for a further 5 seconds. For garlic-flavoured mayonnaise I add 1 clove of peeled, well-crushed, and very finely chopped, garlic to the mayonnaise.

Olive Oil
The original oil for cooking. Some trees, still fruiting, are over 2,000 years old. The best oil, called first cold-press virgin oil, has a wonderful fruity taste.

Traditionally the best oils come from Italy, and the further south in Italy the better. But some Greek oils are excellent. The thicker and greener-looking the oil the better it is likely to taste. Olive oil is high in mono-unsaturated fats and, in reasonable quantities, is positively good for you.

Pancetta
Italian salted pork belly, often herbed, rolled and then air-dried. It can be extremely fatty or rather like our streaky bacon. When rendered, the fat is wonderful for cooking with. Can be used in Italian recipes whenever bacon or salted pork is called for.

Potato
Bear in mind that there are two main types of potato: the *floury* varieties which are best for boiling and mashing; and the *waxy* varieties which are good for potato salad and for frying. Of the two, the waxy varieties are probably better for use in stews, since they keep their shape and do not disintegrate.

Purée
To render solid foods into a mash as in "mashed" potatoes or thick soup. This can be done in a food processor or a mouli-sieve by forcing the food through a fine mesh. The result is a purée.

Ramekin
A small, glazed pottery dish (of a size suitable for an individual soufflé) and sometimes used as a serving dish

for small individual helpings of baked purées of vegetables.

Reduce
To boil down a liquid, thus driving off water, in order to reduce it in quantity and intensify its flavour. See **Deglaze.**

Season
To add salt, pepper or other spices to food to improve the flavour.

Seasoned Flour
Flour to which has been added salt and freshly ground black pepper or other spices.

Shred
To chop finely into thin strips.

Simmer
To cook in liquid just below boiling-point, with the liquid just trembling (96-98°C, 205-209°F). Barely to simmer is to cook at an even lower temperature when the liquid hardly moves at all.

Soy Sauce
A strong sauce fermented from soya beans and much used in Chinese cooking. Light soy sauce is thin and salty and used as a condiment. Rich soy sauce is thicker, stronger-tasting and used during cooking to give extra flavour and a deep rich colour to food.

Stock
Made by adding liquid (usually water) to the bones and flesh of meat (which may or may not have been browned first in the oven) to strongly flavoured vegetables, or to

fish, with added vegetables, herbs and spices. This is cooked slowly to produce a rich-tasting, thin soup which is then strained and stored.

Strain
To separate the liquid from a cooked food usually by the use of a sieve or strainer.

Vinaigrette
The standard salad dressing of three parts oil (olive or walnut) to one part wine vinegar, with a scarce amount of salt and occasionally a tiny amount of spice or other flavouring. This dressing should be well amalgamated and only enough to dress the leaves should be applied (in other words "don't drown it!").

Whip
To beat eggs or cream vigorously until they are frothy and thick from captured air.

Whisk
A looped utensil used to beat air into eggs, cream or batter. The act of using a whisk to whip these foods.

Wine in Cooking
When a recipe in this book calls for wine it specifies white or red. The quality of the wine used for cooking is a matter for you and your purse, but it makes sense to use a small quantity of the wine you intend to drink with the meal. You cannot expect to use "gut-rot" and get away with it. If the wine in the recipe is being used principally to tenderise the meat then it is preferable to use a little good red or white wine vinegar in the marinade rather than a poor-quality wine.

4

Herbs, Spices and Flavourings

You cannot progress beyond basic cooking without a knowledge of herbs, spices and flavourings. And yet it is a subject which is often treated in a cursory way in many cookery books. In many recipes, a herb, a spice, or some other flavouring, like wine or garlic, or a mixture of all three, can be the essential ingredients which transform the dish, which set it apart from another dish with identical basic ingredients.

Herbs are, broadly speaking, green leafy plants which grow in temperate climates, and are used fresh or dried. Spices are the dried, often ground, seeds, root, bark, or stalks, of plants or trees which grow in the tropics. Some plants, like coriander, celery, dill, fenugreek, and lovage, can be used both as herb and as spice. You will often see the phrase "season to taste" in recipe books. This is not deliberate vagueness, but the honest recognition that it is almost impossible to specify the correct amount of any flavouring because taste can vary (as can the taste of other ingredients in the recipe). Dried mint has a completely different taste (and therefore effect) to mint freshly picked from the garden; freshly ground whole black peppercorns are much more pungent and aromatic than ready-ground black pepper bought in a small jar from a supermarket shelf; sea salt has a quite different taste to rock salt and both differ from ordinary cooking salt, which has been refined in a factory and had other ingredients added to it to make it pour. For these reasons, a careful cook tastes a dish, not just before serving it, but throughout its preparation. The time at which a herb, spice or flavouring is added to a dish can have a crucial effect on how the dish tastes. Some flavourings, like ground pepper, mint, parsley and chervil, are fragile and lose their impact if heated for too long.

Some dishes, too, need more flavouring than others. Sauces and stuffings, which usually accompany foods which are in themselves bland, need more flavouring than a soup which is served alone. Steamed fish needs less seasoning than beef stew. Cold food needs more flavouring than hot and chilled or iced dishes even more than cold food served at room temperature. Wherever possible, herbs should be used fresh rather than dried, and spices should be bought whole and ground as required. There are exceptions to this broad generalisation—dried oregano is even better than fresh; turmeric root is so hard that it is best bought ready-ground—but it is a sound basic precept.

HERBS

Today many fresh herbs are widely available; many can be grown in the garden or in pots on a sunny window-sill. Most herbs are at their best before they flower. If you are growing your own, nip out the flower buds to force the plant to continue producing leaves. When buying fresh herbs look for healthy sprigs with a good fragrance and no dried ends, discoloured leaves or wilted stalks. Store fresh herbs with short stalks in an unsealed plastic bag in the fridge for no more than a week. Those with longer stalks can be treated like flowers and put into a small vase or jar with some water.

Fragile Herbs
These are herbs with soft fragile leaves and are at their best when freshly picked, are often eaten raw and should only be cooked lightly. Their leaves bruise easily and they should be only coarsely chopped. These herbs do not dry well for storage, losing much of their pungent flavour and their wonderful aroma.

Parsley
Parsley is the commonest available herb and is rich in vitamins and minerals. Most often used finely chopped as a garnish, it is often used as a substitute for the other fragile herbs without ever matching them in flavour and smell.

Tarragon
One of the classic *fines herbes*, it has particular affinity with chicken and is an essential ingredient in béarnaise sauce. Often used to flavour good wine vinegar.

Mint
Spearmint is the most commonly grown variety for cooking. I grow Bowles mint which is pungent in salads and as an accompaniment to lamb and new potatoes. Much used in Middle Eastern dishes.

Basil
Basil is the classic accompaniment to tomatoes, pungent, aromatic, with a rich, peppery flavour. Basil is the basis for the great Italian *pesto* sauce with pasta.

Chervil
Another of the *fines herbes*, chervil is said to intensify the flavour of other herbs. Never add it to dishes until just before serving. Often chopped and sprinkled on soups and butter sauces.

Borage
A refreshing taste of cucumber means that borage is often used in salads and in fruit punches. Borage goes well with shellfish and I use the lovely blue flowers as a decoration for puddings like syllabub.

Chives
Chives have tubular grass-like leaves and a mild onion flavour. They can be used raw or added to a dish at the end of cooking. The leaves bruise very easily and should be snipped with a scissors rather than chopped with a knife. Often used as a garnish, chives are also added to salads, omelettes and other egg or potato dishes.

Robust Herbs
These herbs have tougher leaves and stand up to cooking well. They are strong in aroma and tend to be harsh-tasting when raw. They dry well.

Thyme
Thyme is almost indispensable for stocks, sauces, stews and slow-cooked braised meats.

Rosemary
Rosemary must be used in moderation although there are many classic Italian dishes which use it as the only herb. It has a strong, sweet smell and a characteristic taste. A sprig of rosemary is a classic accompaniment to roast lamb.

Sage
The traditional herb for sausages and stuffings and felt to have a particular affinity with pork and poultry. Fresh sage has a sweeter, more subtle taste than dried, which I find musty.

Marjoram and Oregano
Closely related, these two are often used interchangeably in cooking. Both are often used fresh in salads and these are the classic herbs in pasta sauces, pizzas and Italian meat stews.

Savory
With slightly larger leaves and a more bitter taste than thyme, savory is often used sprinkled on or cooked with strong-tasting vegetables like cabbage and brussels sprouts, in sausages and stuffings, and is the classic herb to accompany broad beans.

Garlic
A member of the onion family and a wonderful flavouring in food. Fresh garlic is widely available and easy to use. I never buy or use commercially prepared products like garlic salt, garlic purée, garlic pepper or garlic powder. I think they smell dreadful and taste worse.

Fresh garlic is bought by the "bulb" and recipes call for a specified number of "cloves" which are the individual small segments which form the bulb. These should be peeled and the root end and growing tip removed. To do this place the clove on its side on a plate and press down on it with the flat of a knife blade. The tough skin will split allowing the flesh to be removed for use.

SPICES
For hundreds of years spices were the most expensive and most sought-after ingredients. Valued at first for their preserving qualities and their ability to disguise the tainted taste of preserved salted meats, spices are today more valued for their taste and their aroma and are often used to give colour to food. Spices travel well and

deteriorate slowly if they are bought whole and stored out of the light in well-sealed jars, and only ground when needed.

Spices are usually added to a dish right at the start of cooking to allow them to develop their flavour. Many dishes, particularly those from India, often require the spices to be ground and roasted or fried in oil as a preliminary step. This should be done over a low heat to prevent scorching. Spices may be ground by hand with a mortar and pestle, but I keep a separate head of a small electric coffee grinder for spices.

Cumin

A standard ingredient in curried dishes, cumin is much used in North African and in many Middle-Eastern recipes. It can be used whole or ground depending upon the instructions.

Caraway

Caraway seeds need long cooking and they are much used in German and central European breads and cakes as well as in the classic German *sauerkraut* and sausages.

Allspice

Named because its flavour resembles a mixture of cloves, cinnamon and nutmeg, allspice is used in meat mixtures and stews as well as in pastries and some puddings.

Poppy and Sesame Seeds

These are most usually used whole as a sprinkled topping for breads and cakes. Poppy seeds are used in India as a thickening agent in curries and sesame seeds and their oil are used to make tahina, the characteristic flavouring for hummus and other cold purées from the Mediterranean countries.

Clove

Often used in savory stews and more characteristically pushed into onions, roast and baked hams, and baked apples and apple pies. An ingredient (ground) in many Indian spice mixtures.

Cinnamon

Widely used, both whole and ground, cinnamon is a sweet, aromatic spice made from a tree bark. One of the classic pickling spices.

Cardamom

Used in Danish pastries, cooked fruit and Turkish coffee, cardamom is also used extensively in Indian meat and vegetable dishes. Usually sold in the pod, the seeds are separated out as needed, to be ground or used whole.

Juniper Berries

This is the flavouring of gin and other north European alcoholic drinks. Often used in game, stews and with strong vegetables like cabbage.

Nutmeg and Mace

Few spiced cakes or breads taste right without nutmeg and it is much used grated over custards and egg or milk-based puddings and sauces. It goes well with spinach and brussels sprouts. Mace is the outer husk of the fruit and is sweeter and lighter in taste than the central nutmeg seed. Both are best ground or grated as required and used in very small quantities even then.

Paprika and Chilli

Both of these spices come from the fruits of the capsicum family of plants. There are countless varieties which originated in South America, some fiery and red-hot in flavour, others mild and sweet. Red and green sweet peppers are members of the same family and are widely used as vegetables and in salads. The hot flavour comes mainly from the white seeds which cluster round the internal core of the fruit. Paprika, the dried powdered flesh of a sweet, European capsicum, is much milder and gives a rich, red colour to food as well as a sweet, peppery taste. It is the classic ingredient of Hungarian goulash and is much used in Spanish cooking. Chillies come in all shapes, colours and sizes and vary in pungent hotness from sharp and mild to eyeball-popping, mouth-roasting hotness. As a general rule, by no means to be completely relied upon, the smaller, narrower, and deeper in colour the chilli, the more fiery it is likely to be. They can be used fresh or dried and should be used sparingly. When dried, red (ripe) chillies form the basis of cayenne pepper.

Pepper

Black, white and green peppercorns all come from the same plant. Black is the unripe berry, left to dry and darken, white is the ripe berry with the outer casing removed before drying. This results in a less intense flavour. Green peppercorns are the unripe, undried berries and they have a sharp acidic taste and are usually sold preserved in brine. Ground pepper, whether white or black, loses its flavour and aroma rapidly. For that reason it is best ground as required in a mill.

Ginger

Ginger is a root-like rhizome which is used fresh, dried and ground, pickled and even crystallised. It is essential to Asian and a good deal of Indian cooking. It goes well with many fish and shellfish and with strong-tasting poultry and meats. Dried ginger is most used in the baking of cakes and biscuits.

Mustard

Whole mustard seeds are widely used in pickles and relishes, in marinades and in chutneys and in many Indian dishes. When dried and ground mustard must be mixed with water to retain its pungency. Both salt and vinegar have a mollifying effect on ground mustard and so when powdered mustard is used in sauces which contain vinegar or lemon juice it is weaker than when added already mixed with water.

Capers

Capers are the pickled buds of the *Capparis Spinosa* plant and their acidic taste makes them a good foil for rich-tasting meats and fish. Capers are widely used in sauces to accompany cold meats. Heat increases the intensity of their flavour and they should be added only towards the end of cooking.

Recommended Reading

It is beyond the scope of this book to explore the rich and varied uses and particular properties of herbs, spices and flavourings. But two books are essential reading for anyone seriously interested in cooking:

Tom Stobart: *Herbs, Spices and Flavourings* (Penguin Books, 1977)

Elizabeth David: *Spices, Salt and Aromatics in the English Kitchen* (Penguin Books, 1970)

5
Bread

I offer no apology for including a section on breads which can be easily made at home. There is nothing in this world to match the aroma of freshly baked bread and it is the surest way to guests' hearts that I know. I have slaved for days in the kitchen preparing the most elaborate meals only to find that the talking-point at the table was the home-made bread and to have a queue of guests waiting for the recipe before they go home.

It is one of the worst indictments of modern living that good bread, the most basic of foods, is not readily available. No one would suggest that you should make your own cheese or churn your own butter. It is possible to buy fresh vegetables which are almost as good (but never quite) as the dedicated gardener can grow. These foods are as essential to us as bread. Yet, in the stampede to produce foods with endless shelf-life, bread has been the most obvious victim.

Bread with shelf-life is a contradiction in terms. Bread is meant to be eaten fresh. Good bread is the most obvious culinary feature of many other countries. If you are cooking ethnic dishes it makes culinary sense to serve the bread which traditionally accompanies such food. Dipping a piece of soft, bleached, soggy sliced pan into a spicy Indian sauce is not the same experience as dunking a soft *naan*, biting into a crisp *poori*, or tearing off a piece of *chapatti* to act as a spoon. Many of these breads are meant to be eaten hot from the oven or pan. Even if you could buy these breads in ethnic food stores, they just do not have the same taste or texture when reheated.

Once you have mastered the techniques of bread-making you can make any bread—the basic techniques are the same whether you are making *pittas*, Italian *pane integrale*, a wholemeal loaf, or Scotch baps. So, do not be concerned that this section contains recipes for Indian, Italian, Greek, and other ethnic breads as well as for a basic white and brown loaf. It does take a couple of attempts, no more, before you get the feel of a good bread dough into your fingers. Persevere, because once you find your fingers, acquire the knack, baking bread will be one of the easiest as well as one of the most appreciated kitchen tasks. It does not take hours. I get my bread ready to prove while the breakfast kettle boils. I use the food processor.

The ingredients for making good bread are simple: flour, liquid (usually water), a small quantity of fat, salt, a pinch of sugar, and leavening (usually yeast). The method, too, is simple: activate the leavening agent; add it with the liquid to the flour, fat and salt; knead the dough; allow it to prove; bake it; eat it. I tell you this now to prevent you being put off by the detailed explanations which follow. Baking bread is easy—far easier than many recipes you would attempt without so much as a second thought. The rewards are out of all proportion to the effort involved.

Leavening (Raising) Agents

To leaven a bread is to lighten it by introducing bubbles of gas which expand during cooking. The gluten in the flour expands elastically to contain the gas and is then set during cooking. The first breads were probably unleavened and flat, like *chapattis*, *tortillas* or *matzos*.

However, if dough is left for a few hours in warm surroundings, the organisms which are naturally present, including yeasts, will cause fermentation. This natural leavening is still used, for instance, in India. There is an element of chance in this, because the necessary organisms might not be present, and so it became customary to keep back a piece of one batch of successfully risen dough to inoculate the next batch. This starter was known as the leaven. Since the dough became sour through the action of lactic-acid organisms, this bread became known as sour-dough bread. It is still a common technique in eastern European countries and in parts of America.

Nowadays, yeast is usually added as a separate ingredient. For predictable, consistent results buy plain dried baker's yeast in a sealed tin. DCL and Allisons are two reliable and widely available brands. Most brands of quick-action yeasts also contain various improvers and additives (commonly used in large-scale bread production) which, to my taste, produce a flavour akin to shop breads. I feel that this rather defeats the object of the exercise. They work well enough with the recipes on the packets but all the bread recipes in this book use plain dried yeast granules. By all means use fresh yeast if you can get it but it will only keep in good condition for about two weeks in a fridge and three months if frozen. Dried yeast, if carefully sealed after use, will keep well for a long time.

The use of chemical raising agents like bicarbonate of soda, buttermilk and sour milk, was an alternative to yeast before the advent of dried active yeasts. The classic Irish griddle and soda breads rely on this method.

FLOURS

Bread can be, and still is, made from many different grains: wheat, rye, oats, barley and even from flour made from pulses. In western Europe wheat flour is the most widely used.

For bread-making you need *strong* flour, which is, in fact, a combination of locally grown *soft* wheat grains and imported *hard* grains, mainly from the prairies of America and Canada. The hard wheats, ripened in sunnier climates, give the dough better expansion, absorb more water, and you get a better structured loaf. If you use ordinary soft flours, whether white or wholemeal, you will get bread which is heavier in texture. This is true whether the flour is labelled household, cream or pastry flour. These flours are fine for cakes and pastries. Some *strong* flours are bleached and contain "improver" and other additives. Sadly, this is just a case of flour millers responding to the demand for strong flour for home bread-making and packing industrial flours in small packets.

Strong White Flour

This will normally be labelled: 70-73% extraction. Make sure that it is unbleached. This produces a creamy-coloured bread of strong flavour.

Strong 80-85% Wheatmeal Flour

These flours are usually sold under proprietary brand names. They are excellent for biscuits and pastry. Despite what some of the packets say, they also make good bread which is lighter in texture than wholemeal flour bread but has slightly less flavour. For this reason the recipes in this book will stipulate strong white, wholemeal and mixtures of these two flours.

Wholemeal Flour
This contains 100% of the grain. Most people settle for the stone-ground flours which tend to be soft flours. These can be used mixed with strong white flour, or on their own, when they will produce a fairly dense but very tasty loaf.

Salt
All bread needs some salt. Only the Italians and the Chinese like bread with very little or no salt. Exact amounts vary, but roughly two teaspoons of salt to every 500 g of flour is a good rough guide. If you use sea salt, as I do, then it should be dissolved in part of the water allowance before being added to the dough. Commercial table salt can be added directly to the flour.

Fat
Not all breads need added fat but many are actually improved by the addition of a small amount in the form of olive oil, vegetable oil, butter or cream. In Italian breads a good olive oil adds a wonderful flavour. Use small quantities—two tablespoons to each 500 g of flour for a basic loaf.

Liquids
For most breads plain water is all that is necessary. Irish soda breads use soured milk or buttermilk. Some English and Scottish breads use milk. Some Indian breads use yoghurt.

A Basic Loaf

500 g strong flour
2 tsp dried yeast
1 tsp salt
1-2 tbsp vegetable oil, melted butter or cream
300 ml water

(The exact amount of water depends on the absorbency of the flour. If you use a food processor you may need slightly less liquid.)

Put the yeast into two tablespoons of warm water, stir, then leave in a warm place for 10 minutes to activate. (A small pinch of sugar is often added to the mixture to feed the yeast but this is not really necessary with dried active yeast granules.) The yeast is ready when all the granules have dissolved and there is a good head of froth on the surface.

Mix together the flour, salt and fat in the bowl of the food processor. (An ordinary mixing bowl if you are making it by hand.) Put this in a warm place if the weather is cold. A Dutch-oven at its lowest heat setting is ideal.

When the yeast is ready, place the bowl back on the plinth of the food processor and add the yeast mixture to the flour. Activate the processor, and pour in about three-quarters of the water in a controlled, continuous stream. Process until the dough forms a ball and rides on the blade. If it doesn't do this after 30 seconds add a little more water. Process for at least 30 seconds more after the ball of dough rides on the blade. Switch off the machine and feel the dough with your fingers. It should have a silky feel. It is difficult to describe this texture but you will recognise it. Dough that is insufficiently processed will be sticky and lumpy. If the dough has too much water it will be very sticky and sprawl. Just add some more flour and process for another 30 seconds. It is not essential, but I find it helpful, to allow the dough to rest for a few minutes before giving it another 30 seconds processing. For those working the dough by hand, there is no alternative but to keep at it until it becomes elastic and silky in texture. This can take anywhere between 10 and 15 minutes. The dough achieves this consistency quite suddenly as you knead. Once this change has been experienced it is never forgotten. You'll wonder what the problem was.

The bread must now be put to prove. If the room is warm this can be done in the processor bowl. Leave on the lid. If you are working the dough by hand, cover it with a damp cloth or a sheet of stretch polythene wrap. It should stand in a reasonably warm place. In spring, summer and early autumn, room temperature is fine. For the rest of the year, in our draughty, unheated house, I set the bowl on the lid of the Dutch-oven which is set to its lowest temperature. This makes the lid just warm to the touch. I use this method if I want a quick proving—making the dough mid-morning for a mid-afternoon baking. For someone who works away from home, prepare the dough the evening before, let it prove in a cool place overnight, knock it down in the morning and let it prove for a second time while you are at work. This second proving is not essential but can improve the structure of the finished loaf.

The final proving is done in the tin in which the bread will be cooked (or with the dough shaped into a round or a sausage-shape), in a warm place for about 45 minutes to an hour. If you are using the long-rising method then it is a good idea to brush the surface of the dough with oil to prevent a dry crust forming. Most bread recipes refer to the dough doubling in size but don't become paranoid about this. As long as it looks a good deal bigger than when you set it to prove, it will be perfectly edible. The whole purpose of the double rising is to allow the second kneading (which is nothing like so arduous as the first) to redistribute the gases about the bread to get an even structure.

Preheat the oven to 220°C (425°F, gas mark 7). Use an oven thermometer to check this. Baking-time depends on the shape you like your bread. I usually shape it into an oblong sausage shape about ten inches long and place it on an oiled baking tray. But it can be given its final rise in what is still known, even in these metric times, as a two-pound loaf tin. How you shape it is entirely up to you. If you like really crusty bread divide it into two smaller eight-inch sausage shapes. Cut three diagonal slashes in the top of these to a depth of about half an inch with a very sharp knife. Allow a minute or two for these to expand and open up before you put the loaves into the oven.

Two small loaves will take roughly 30 minutes to bake. One big loaf will take 35-40 minutes. If you use an oiled tin allow 45 minutes. Turn down the oven to 190°C (375°F, gas mark 5) after 15 minutes. The bread is done when it sounds hollow when tapped lightly on its base with your knuckles. Lightly is the operative word—even an undercooked loaf will sound hollow if you thump it hard enough. If you cook the bread in a tin, it is normal to slip it out of the tin, and lay it on its side for the last 10 minutes of the cooking-time to allow the bottom crust to firm.

If all of this sounds complicated, believe me—it's not. It takes more time to write about than to do. Fit the proving time round everything else you must do. An hour, here or there, will not make much difference to the proving.

Wholemeal Loaf

The method for making this wholemeal loaf is identical to that for the basic loaf. Mix strong wholemeal flour with strong white flour in whatever proportions suit your taste. I recommend at least 20% white flour because a yeast-leavened loaf made from wholemeal flour alone can be extremely dense and solid, almost unpalatable. Somewhere between the ratios 1-4 and 1-1 parts white to wholemeal flour is the loaf to suit your taste. Proportions and ingredients, other than the flour, are exactly the same as for the basic loaf.

You will come across recipes for a wholemeal bread using the no-knead (and short proving) method. Unless you are an addict of wholemeal flour bread (without the addition of any strong white) I do not recommend them. These recipes all produce heavy, slab-like loaves which are a penance to eat.

Pitta Breads

This very popular bread originated in the Middle East and comes in two types. The basic dough is the same for both, but the cooking method determines whether the cooked pitta is a small, flat, rather chewy pocket in which to stuff various fillings (like the frozen commercial pittas widely available in supermarkets), or a flat bread without a pocket which is served at table. Each has its place and I give the method for both types.

500 g strong white flour
300 ml warm water (approx.)
1 tbsp good olive oil
1 heaped tsp dried yeast

Follow the method for a basic loaf dough, whether you are using a food processor or working the dough by hand. Set the dough to prove in a warm place. When it has roughly doubled in size, knock it down and knead by hand for about 5 minutes.

To make hollow pocket pittas:

Divide the dough into nine equal pieces. These should be roughly the size of a large egg. On a floured surface, roll out each ball of dough until it is a flat oval shape about ½cm thick. Cover each bread with a floured or a damp cloth while you roll out the others. If you are baking them in the oven you should lay them out on flat, lightly oiled baking trays. You will fit three on a rectangular tray. If you are going to cook them on a pan on top of the cooker lay them out on a flat surface. Let them prove for 10-15 minutes.

Oven method:
Preheat the oven to 220°C (425°F, gas mark 7). Place one baking tray on the top shelf of the oven and cook the breads for about 8 minutes. This is one sure way to find out how even your oven temperature is. If it is even all three breads should have puffed up all over like balloons and be lightly tinged with brown. If this has been successful remove this batch and keep them warm while you cook the other two batches. If you have a fan-assisted oven or a gas gyro-flow oven you should be able to cook all of the breads together using three shelves. They can be eaten at once while still warm or they can be left to cool and then deep-frozen. To reheat them when frozen, place the frozen pitta in the microwave. Switch on the oven at full power. After about 40 seconds, the pitta will begin to puff. Switch off the oven, turn the pitta over and give it a final belt until it puffs completely. This method of reheating frozen pittas works for the pan-cooked ones and shop-bought ones too. Much the same results can be got under a hot grill if you do not have a microwave.

Pan Method:
Lightly oil a large, heavy-bottomed frying-pan and heat it on top of the cooker until it is very hot. Place one pitta in the centre of the pan. Leave it until it puffs up all over. Turn it over quickly and cook for less time on the other side. The whole process takes about 2½-3 minutes. You can cook these under the grill as well. These methods

produce a slightly chewy, doughier-tasting pitta than oven-cooking. They are closer in flavour and texture to the commercial varieties. Which you prefer is a matter of taste. Opinions are evenly divided in our household.

To make Flat Bread (Solid) Pittas:
Divide the dough into six even-sized pieces. Roll them out into oval shapes about 1-1½ cm thick. Place the breads on lightly oiled baking trays. Brush the top surface of each bread with water and cover with a damp cloth. Leave them to prove for 25-30 minutes. Preheat the oven to 220°C (425°F, gas mark 7). Bake the pittas for 10-15 minutes depending on thickness. They do not puff and should brown only slightly. They are cooked when they sound hollow when tapped. These pittas should be eaten hot from the oven. They will keep, in the Dutch-oven or another warm place, for 10-15 minutes. They become rather chewy if eaten cold and they go stale overnight. They do not freeze or reheat successfully.

Italian Focaccia
Focaccia is a delicious Italian flat bread. It is best eaten hot from the oven but is also delicious when cooled and split lengthways to make sandwiches with Italian raw ham or salami.

The name comes from the latin *focus* or hearth, and focaccia was a bread baked on a bakestone at the hearth. Nowadays it is baked in a bread oven. In Italy focaccia comes in two types: one large flat bread about two inches thick with various flavourings, and a smaller, thinner variety which Italians buy in individual servings and eat fresh from the baker's on their way to and from work. These smaller varieties are often flavoured with onion, herbs, olives, or *pancetta* (Italian fat bacon) and are a meal in themselves. The larger loaves are eaten at home as an accompaniment to a meal, or split and made into delicious sandwiches with many different fillings. Focaccia is a white bread. Although I am sure you could make a wholemeal version of it, I have never seen this done or suggested. Commercially baked focaccia is not available in this country (to my knowledge) and so you must make this at home. It is well worth the effort.

400 g strong white flour
2 tsp dried yeast
5 tbsp good olive oil
4 tbsp water
2 tsp salt
a good pinch of sea salt for topping

To bake focaccia successfully you will need a baking-stone (I use quarry tiles) about 12-14 inches long and 9 inches wide, which can be preheated in the oven. It is never quite as successful (though perfectly acceptable) when baked on a thin metal baking tray.

Activate the dried yeast in 4 tablespoons of warm water. When it has formed a good head of froth add it to the flour in the bowl of the food processor with 2½ tablespoons of the olive oil. Process for about a minute until the dough rides on the blade. Set it to prove in a warm place for about three hours. It should more than double in size. Knock it down and knead again by hand for 3-5 minutes. Roll the dough out to a rectangle (or a circle) about 12-14 inches long and 10 inches wide. The size is not critical. The bread should be about 1½ inches thick. Use your forefinger and thumb to pinch up the edges and the surface of the dough. This gives a dimple effect with a slight raising at the edges to retain the olive oil (1½ tbsp) which you now trickle all over the surface of the dough. Sprinkle a good pinch of coarse sea salt over the surface.

Bake, directly on the hot bakestone, in a preheated oven at 220°C (425°F, gas mark 7) for about 15-20 minutes depending upon thickness. The oil is absorbed into the bread and forms a rich, dark, golden-brown crust. Serve hot from the oven for preference, or while still warm. If you want to use it cold, do not store it in the fridge. This is the basic plain, salty focaccia.
Variations:
There are many traditional Italian variations.

Herb Focaccia
Add 1½ tablespoons of freshly chopped herb (traditionally rosemary or sage) to the dough while kneading it after its initial proving. Sprinkle ½ tablespoonful of the herb with a pinch of salt over the surface of the bread with the oil.

Focaccia with Pancetta
3-4 oz of uncooked fatty *pancetta* (Italian air-dried and herbed bacon) can be chopped into very small cubes and incorporated into the dough during the second kneading.

Focaccia with Onions
Peel and slice an onion, separate into rings and soak them in water while the bread is proving. Dry the onion rings on kitchen paper and press them very lightly onto the surface of the bread before baking. Add the oil and salt after the onion rings.

Indian Chapattis
A favourite unleavened Indian bread which is simplicity itself to make at home. Chapattis are torn apart at table and used to carry sauces and rice to your mouth with your fingers.

100 g finely ground wholemeal flour
50 g flour for rolling the breads
120 ml (6 floz) water

Put the main flour into the bowl of the food processor (or an ordinary bowl if you are making the chapattis by hand) and add enough water while the processor is on to form a dough which rides on the blade after about a minute's processing. Allow the dough to stand for at least half an hour, covered with a damp cloth. Divide the dough into 6-8 small pieces and roll each into a ball in your hands. Flour a flat surface with a sprinkle of the remaining flour and flour the rolling pin. Take one of the balls of dough and dip it into the flour. Now roll it out into a thin circle of about 10-12 centimetres. Keep the surfaces of the chapatti and the rolling pin well floured. Set each chapatti aside as you roll it out.

Heat a dry, heavy-bottomed frying-pan over a medium heat until it is very hot, almost smoking. Place a chapatti on the pan. Within about 30 seconds, bubbles will appear on the upper surface. Turn the chapatti over and cook for another 30 seconds.

You need a gas flame for the next stage. If you do not have a gas cooker you could use a camping-gas burner. This will not work on an electric ring. Lift the chapatti with a tongs and place it directly onto the gas flame. Almost at once it will swell alarmingly and puff up into a ball. Remove it from the flame and place it on a plate. Now spread one surface with butter. (If you want to be really correct it should be clarified butter or ghee.) Cook all the chapattis in this way and place them on top of each other in a folded envelope of cooking-foil, in a low oven, to keep warm. They keep this way for about 30 minutes.

Indian Naan Breads

This leavened, flat Indian bread is the perfect accompaniment to a *tandoori* dish but is also good with any other grilled or barbecued foods.

- 500 g strong white flour
- 150 ml (5 floz) milk
- 1 beaten egg
- 1 tsp salt
- 1 tsp sugar
- 1½ tsp dried yeast
- 1 tsp baking powder
- 4 tbsp plain (unsweetened) yoghurt
- 2 tbsp vegetable oil
- 1 tsp black onion seeds (*kalonji*) or poppy seeds

Warm four tablespoons of the milk in a bowl and activate the yeast in this with a pinch of the sugar. Put the flour, beaten egg, salt, sugar, baking powder, oil and yoghurt into the bowl of the food processor. When the yeast is frothy add it to this mixture. Process, adding just enough of the remaining milk to get the ball of dough to ride on the blade. If you are working the dough by hand it will take at least 10 minutes kneading for the dough to become silky and elastic. Let the dough prove for 2-3 hours. (It can stand longer in a cooler place.)

Divide the dough into six even pieces and work each of these with your fingers into tear-shaped pieces about 10-12 inches long and 4 inches wide. Place them on a lightly oiled baking tray and cover them with a damp cloth. Let them prove again for 15-20 minutes. Preheat the oven to 220°C (425°F, gas mark 7). Just before baking brush the top surface of each *naan* with water (or milk) and sprinkle on the onion or poppy seeds. Bake for 12-15 minutes. They remain rather pale breads with slightly crisp bases and very tender centres. They must be eaten hot from the oven.

Traditionally, *naans* are cooked in the tremendous dry heat of the *tandoor* clay oven. It is possible to grill *naans* and they will puff slightly and become chewy rather than meltingly soft like the oven-baked breads.

IRISH SODA BREAD

Neither of these breads needs a food processor or any kneading or proving because they rely upon chemical raising agents whose action is lost if the dough is left longer than three minutes after mixing.

Brown Soda Bread (Cake)

500 g flour
1 tsp bicarbonate of soda
1 tsp salt
300 ml buttermilk, sour milk or whey

Use a half-and-half mixture of white and wholemeal flour. Mix this with the salt and the bicarbonate of soda in a wide bowl. Make a well in the centre and pour in about half of the buttermilk. Using a round-bladed knife quickly draw the flour into the liquid. Keep adding liquid until almost all the flour has been gathered into a sloppy dough. Gently and quickly knead in the last of the flour in the bowl. You want to end up with a soft dough but, depending on the flour, may not need all of the liquid. Turn the dough out onto a floured board and quickly shape it and knead it into a circle without cracks which is about an inch and a half (7-8 cm) thick.

Do not be tempted to knead the bread in the manner you would knead yeast bread. It is not necessary. The whole process from the moment you add the buttermilk to the ingredients in the bowl should take no more than 3 minutes. Any longer and the action of the bicarbonate of soda is lost. Bake on a floured baking-sheet or in a floured cast-iron pot at 200°C (400°F, gas mark 6) for 35–40 minutes. The bread should be lightly browned and sound hollow when tapped on the bottom with your knuckles. Turn out onto a rack to cool. This is the basic traditional recipe.

Griddle Bread (White Soda Bread)

In our house this is known as Dinky's Bread in honour of a dear friend who was joint mother to our son. When he was born I was an actress in a weekly television drama series. I had little choice but to go back to work one week after he was born. Dinky (Anna) Heffernan, now sadly dead, was a fine actress from an old theatrical family, who had travelled the halls of rural Ireland "fitting-up" night after night. She had raised three fine sons herself and she stepped into the breach when my son was born. She became his "second" mother. When I arrived back from work to collect him I would be greeted by a happy, smiling child and, invariably, a loaf of fresh griddle bread to take with me. I can smell it yet. She cooked it every day of her life. It shows how great the love of fresh home-made bread is in Ireland if you think of the terrible difficulties she must have had to do so while "on the road." She cooked it on top of an old-fashioned paraffin stove because she said its gentle heat made the best bread. The stove was kept solely for this purpose long after the need for it as a heater had passed. It remains my son's favourite bread, to be eaten for breakfast with grilled smoked rashers from the inimitable Jack Hick of Sallynoggin.

Follow the instructions for brown soda bread in the previous recipe but use only plain white flour. It is only the cooking method which is different. Heat the griddle or a large flat pan over a medium heat. Roll out the dough, quickly and gently, into a circle about 1½ inches thick. Score it into four pointers or farls. You can separate them or leave them touching. As soon as you put the bread onto the griddle turn the heat down to very low and allow the bread to cook for 5 minutes. It will rise and form a light dry skin on the upper surface. Turn the heat up again (not too much) and cook until it is lightly browned underneath. Turn the bread over and cook at the same heat on the other side. The whole operation will take from 30 to 40 minutes depending on the heat under the griddle.

Some people like to eat their griddle bread hot, with lashings of butter; some allow it to cool on a wire rack, others wrap it in a clean cloth to cool and this gives it a softer crust. Leftovers can be fried for breakfast in bacon fat. Split the farl down the centre and fry until crisp and golden-brown.

Milk Rolls

These are soft white bread rolls and their great advantage is that they freeze well without loss of texture. I use them to make filled rolls for packed lunches. If taken from the freezer first thing in the morning they are completely thawed by lunch-time.

500 g strong white flour (or a 50/50 mixture of white and wholemeal)
1½ tsp dried yeast
2 tsp salt
2 tbsp olive oil or vegetable oil
300 ml (50/50 mixture) of milk and water

Warm the milk and water mixture to a tepid heat and reactivate the yeast in a bowl with a small amount of it. Warm the flour a little. This can be done in the microwave for about 10 seconds, or in the Dutch-oven. When the yeast is frothy put all the ingredients into the bowl of the food processor and process for about 1 minute until the dough forms a ball and rides on the blade. This dough is slacker than most of the bread doughs we have made up to now. If you are kneading it by hand, this means that it will not require as much time before the texture turns. Cover and let it prove until it has doubled in size.

Knock down the dough and knead again by hand on a floured surface for about 3 minutes. Divide the dough into eight equal pieces. Knead each of these until smooth and place them on a lightly oiled baking tray. Flatten them gently with your fingers until they are all of even height and diameter. Cover them with a damp cloth or an oiled sheet of cling-film. Leave to rise for 15-20 minutes. Bake in a preheated oven at 200°C (400°F, gas mark 6) for about 15 minutes. If your oven is uneven in temperature you may need to turn the tray to ensure even cooking. Allow them to cool on a rack. Eat these cold.

6

The Fifteen-minute Marathon

Reconciling your desire for real food with a hard day's work and the nightly toil through the rush-hour traffic is difficult. It's so easy to nip in to the local 24-hour shop to pick up a "gourmet ready-to-eat dinner for one" or to stop by at the local takeaway for a pizza "straight from our gas-fired, traditional wood oven"; easier still to find an excuse to call in to that interesting pub which advertises "drink'n'eat happy hours." Nothing wrong with that once in a while. But, with a little forethought you could conjure up a meal fit for a gourmet in fifteen minutes.

Nothing, from the simplest, most devastating advertising campaign to the marvellous little black cocktail dress you ran up in half an hour just before leaving for the party, is ever as simple as it looks—it's all in the planning. That advertising campaign had been skulking round the periphery of your brain for years waiting for the right client or product to come along; the material from which you knocked up the devastating little number had been carefully selected at a remnant day sale two years ago.

It's the same with fifteen-minute gourmet food. You need a three-pronged attack: keep a reasonable supply of quickly prepared food in your deep-freeze; double-cook on days when you have the urge and time to prepare favourite foods; find good, reliable, knowledgeable suppliers of ready-to-eat foods.

While we have nothing to approach the French *charcuterie* there are a growing number of specialist shops which prepare and stock high-quality ready-to-eat foods.

Cheese

Finding out about cheeses is one of the great joys of learning about food. There are literally thousands of different cheeses, each with its own unique texture, taste and smell. Seek out a retailer who likes cheese, one who will talk to you about it rather than just sell it to you, because cheese, more than almost any other product, needs to be loved and understood. Cheese is like wine; it has countless varieties. You can move a master cheesemaker with all his secrets and skills to another locality and he will be unable to make the same cheese because the grass and herbage on which the cows, sheep or goats feed is different, because the water is different, the climate is slightly different, or because the bacteria in the air are different.

Buy a good book about cheese and read it. Like wine, cheese has its classic literature. *The Cheese Book* by Vivienne Marquis and Patricia Haskell is an excellent primer.

There is a growing farm-cheese movement in this country. While these cheeses do cost more than the average "factory" cheese, in most cases they are worth it. It is worth remembering that although many cheeses from abroad look, taste and smell more exotic than locally produced farm cheeses, many of those which reach this country are actually factory-produced cheeses. The farm cheesemakers in this country are struggling to develop a varied and interesting range of native cheeses. Without the encouragement and support of native consumers they cannot hope to succeed.

Basic Rules

Serve all cheese at room temperature. Hard cheeses take longer to reach this temperature than soft cheeses.

Buy, cut and serve only as much cheese as you expect to use. No cheese responds well to re-refrigeration. Do not place strong and mild cheeses close to each other. Have a separate knife for cutting each cheese. Offer a choice of cheese but don't overdo it. Two really good, contrasting cheeses which strike a balance between strong and mild flavours are better than a proliferation of inferior ones. Offer a choice of beverage with cheese. Don't be tempted to decorate cheese with bits of pineapple, cherries, or sprigs of herbs. Offer crisp herbs like watercress, or celery sticks, gherkins, or pickled onions separately. A good home-baked Italian bread is always better than salted crackers. Store cheese if possible in a cool place that is not the fridge. If you must use a fridge then store the cheese at the bottom just above the vegetable drawer. Always keep cheese well wrapped in greaseproof paper or foil rather than cling-film.

Cured, Smoked and Pickled Fish

Smoked salmon, smoked trout, smoked eel, and smoked mackerel, which is more robust in flavour but considerably less expensive, are all widely available and provide the basis for an almost instant meal.

Smoked Salmon

There are two ways of buying this: pre-sliced and vacuum-packed, or sliced from a whole side in a specialist shop.

The vacuum-packed salmon is usually of reasonable quality but is often farmed fish rather than wild salmon. However, it does have the advantage that it can be stored, unopened in the fridge, for a considerable time against an emergency.

The wild salmon is traditionally smoked over oak and a good side of salmon will have a slightly oily sheen and look moist. The outer layer always has a dried appearance and is sliced on the diagonal so that a small rim of this outer layer is incorporated into each slice, to prevent waste. You can buy a whole side or a number of slices. It is quite difficult to slice evenly and so, if you are going to eat the salmon quickly, ask the fishmonger to slice it for you. Don't be tempted to buy more than you need. It is very rich and expensive.

The best-quality salmon is perfectly accompanied by good brown bread and butter, a quarter of lemon, and a crisp green salad.

Smoked Salmon with Scrambled Eggs

This is a marvellous meal which takes no time to prepare at any time of the day. Perfect for breakfast entertaining but equally good late at night in front of the fire.

Serves 2:

100 g sliced smoked salmon
4 eggs
60 g butter
30 ml cream

2 tsp chopped fresh dill leaves
salt and freshly ground black pepper (to taste)

Serves 6:

300 g sliced smoked salmon
12 eggs
120 g butter
90 ml cream
6 tsp chopped fresh dill leaves
salt and freshly ground black pepper (to taste)

Heat the butter in a heavy-bottomed pot over a gentle heat. Whisk the eggs with the cream until they are combined and frothy. Season. Pour them into the pot with the butter and cook them gently, stirring constantly along the bottom of the pot at first, then, as they begin to coagulate, up the sides as well. When the eggs are creamy, but still thinner than you want to serve them, remove the pot from the heat. Continue stirring until they reach the consistency you like. Serve them at once, sprinkled with the chopped dill, alongside the smoked salmon. Brown bread and butter to accompany them.

Smoked Trout

Trout, like salmon, are farmed extensively today. Most of the smoked trout available in the shops is farmed trout, usually rainbow trout. Like salmon, the wild brown trout and the sea-trout (white trout) tend to be smaller and better flavoured. These should be purchased whenever you see them but are increasingly difficult to get. If you know a fisherman it might be an idea to get fish from him and smoke them yourself with a small smoking unit. There are several types available and, used with care, they can be extremely successful.

Commercial brands of smoked trout usually come

unpacked, complete with head. Sea-trout, which is more delicate in flavour, is more often headless, filleted, and vacuum-packed.

Remove the head from the trout—it will twist off easily—and remove any remaining bones. You can remove the skin before serving if you like. Treat exactly as you would smoked salmon or serve with a lightly flavoured creamed horseradish sauce.

Horseradish Sauce

Serves 2 :

1 tbsp freshly grated horseradish root
1 dsrtsp wine vinegar
75 ml fresh cream, lightly whipped
salt and freshly ground black pepper (to taste)

Serves 6:

3 tbsp freshly grated horseradish root
1 tbsp wine vinegar
225 ml fresh cream, lightly whipped
salt and freshly ground black pepper (to taste)

Horseradish root is hot and powerful and a whiff of it can reduce strong men to tears. This is why so much ready prepared, creamed horseradish sauce is bought. This is usually the grated root preserved in vinegar and, despite the label's claims to the contrary, is not ready to serve from the jar. Mix it with cream at the rate of 1 teaspoonful of creamed horseradish to 30 ml cream. It does make an acceptable substitute for the real thing but the real thing can transform your trout into a talking-point.

Wash the root and peel off the outer skin. Cut the root into chunks. Drop these into the food processor and process them until they are very finely grated. Avert your face when you remove the lid. The tear-inducing aroma dissipates quite quickly so that it is possible to be close to the grated root but the fact that it does so explains why the commercial variety is not a patch on the real sauce. Add the grated root to the other ingredients and serve in a chilled bowl.

Smoked Eel and Smoked Mackerel

Eel and mackerel have robust, distinctive flavours and are very oily fish. They stand up well to horseradish or even plain lemon juice. With a sharp green salad and good wholemeal bread they make a healthy and very quick meal.

Pickled or Marinated Fish

It is possible to buy an increasing variety of ready-to-eat fish in specialist shops. These range from the dill-flavoured pickled salmon *gravad lax* to the humble, but no less delicious, roll-mop herring. All these fish are very good for you and can be quickly served with a crunchy salad to set off the softer texture of the fish. Try eating these northern pickled fish with a bread based on rye flour.

Gravad Lax

For each serving (the smaller amount as a starter)

60-100 g dill-pickled salmon
1-2 tbsp Scandinavian mustard sauce

The pickled salmon should be thinly sliced liked smoked salmon. Some vacuum-packed brands come with a ready-made sauce but I find this too sweet and cloying. Make up the sauce which follows or serve it with soured cream flavoured with chopped fresh dill leaves.

Scandinavian Mustard Sauce

Serves 2:

100 ml mayonnaise
½ tbsp brown sugar
¾ tbsp Dijon mustard
¾ tbsp chopped capers
¾ tbsp chopped gherkin
1 anchovy fillet (chopped)
1 tbsp fresh dill

Serves 6-8:

400 ml mayonnaise
2 tbsp brown sugar
3 tbsp Dijon mustard
3 tbsp chopped capers
3 tbsp chopped gherkin
3 chopped anchovy fillets
3 tbsp chopped fresh dill leaves

Add all the ingredients except the dill to a bowl and stir them until well mixed. Add the dill and mix lightly.

Pickled Herring

There are two basic methods of pickling herrings and endless variations on each. The trick is to find a pickle which is to your taste. Roll-mop herrings are not cooked, but salted before pickling in vinegar. Herrings can also be cooked in a vinegar pickle and are often called, erroneously, soused herrings but are really baked herrings. The vinegar, the spices and the other ingredients vary wildly and can have a remarkable effect on the taste. Most European countries have their own favourite, often secret recipes. My husband is a Scotsman and was reared on pickles based on strong malt vinegars. I find these impossibly harsh and prefer the gentler taste of wine or cider vinegars. If you are buying pickled fish of any kind from a shop ask if you can taste a piece before you buy. It's a perfectly reasonable request. All pickled fish can be served as a starter or as a main course. They are quick, delicious and need nothing more than good bread and butter and a salad to make a very healthy meal.

Barbecued Salmon
This is a new invention by an Irish company based in Co. Limerick. The fish is smoked at a higher than usual temperature and basted during smoking with a marinade. The result is distinctive and delicious. It is sold already sliced and vacuum-packed and can be eaten cold or briefly cooked in a microwave.

Cured Meats

These divide into two distinct groups: the great traditional cured meats, which are sometimes smoked and usually eaten raw, and the more recent inventions, often just cooked meats, which have been given a decorative smoking.

The best-known traditional cures are the hams from Westphalia in Germany, Parma in Italy, Bayonne in France, and Spanish *jamón serrano*. In mainland Europe there are many local cures, often called country hams, which can be well worth seeking out when you are on holiday. At home, it can be worth looking for an expatriate pork butcher from Germany or Italy or one who specialises in German or Italian pork products. They may well have their own version of cured ham, but may also experiment with other meats like beef or venison, and may make smoked or cured sausages which will be in an altogether different class to the factory varieties commonly available.

Prosciutto

Italian *prosciutto crudo* (raw ham) is not smoked but carefully, lovingly, dry-salted and air-dried, certainly for months, often for up to two years. I know of no greater pleasure than the first of the new season *prosciutto* served out of doors in late summer with fresh green figs, melon or pears, freshly baked bread from a wood oven and sweet butter. That from Parma is the most famous, and expensive, but the local cures can be just as exciting, often saltier, more robust in flavour but just as wonderful. *Prosciutto* should be very thinly sliced but not paper-thin and translucent.

Westphalian Ham

This most famous German ham is dry-salted, brined and then smoked over beechwood and juniper berries. Always eaten raw, its strong, smoky flavour is best appreciated alone, with good brown bread and butter and a twist of black pepper. Other German hams can be served with a creamed horseradish sauce or a variety of pickled vegetables, or pickled pears, and strong rye bread.

Jamón Serrano

Most Spanish hams are best avoided. But *jamón serrano* (mountain ham) made from the black Iberian pig which runs free in the high forests (and is therefore very lean) is a dry-salted ham which is then lightly brined before being hung to dry through the winter. It is not smoked, and though tougher than Italian, French or German hams of similar quality is very fine in flavour. Serve with good olives and bread.

Jambon de Bayonne

This French ham is lightly smoked and always eaten raw. But there are many good French hams from other regions which can be smoked or unsmoked, eaten raw or cooked.

Cured Beef and Venison

An odd coupling you might think, but the flavour of cured beef and venison is not dissimilar—slightly sweet and strong. The Italian cured beef *bresaola* is a whole fillet of beef, dry-salted and air-dried, with a flavour that is sharper and yet more delicate than cured ham. Swiss *grison* is often pressed into a more regular shape but is similar in flavour. There is an Irish smoked beef which is stronger in flavour than either of these. Venison and reindeer (which you will come across occasionally) are not unlike beef with just a hint of a gamey sweetness. They make a great guessing game at table. I like them both.

Cured Sausages

There are so many varieties of these, both imported and home produced, good, bad and positively vile, that the only way of discovering which you like is to eat small quantities of as many as possible and keep notes of the names of those you like and those you will avoid for ever more.

The very best education is to eat as many varieties as possible when you are abroad and then look and ask for those you like when you come home. As a rough rule of thumb, a small producer with an ethnic connection is more likely to be producing a sausage which bears some relation to its continental original. Factory-produced sausages can usually be recognised by their uniform geometric shape and in my experience can vary in taste from the reasonable to the positively awful. This goes for both foreign and home-based manufacturers. The genuine article is rarely completely symmetrical and some can look downright ugly. Price can be another guide. You cannot expect to buy real sausage or salami for the same price as luncheon roll.

Quick Starters

Avocado Pear and Smoked Salmon

Serves 2:

1 avocado pear
60 g smoked salmon
1 tbsp lemon juice or vinaigrette made with lemon juice

Serves 6:

3 avocado pears
200 g smoked salmon
3 tbsp lemon juice or vinaigrette made with lemon juice

Cut the slices of salmon up into thin slivers. Halve the avocado, remove the stone and peel off the skin carefully and thinly. Place the avocado halves face down on a serving dish and slice them. Brush each half with the lemon juice or vinaigrette to prevent discoloration. Just before serving, sprinkle the salmon over the avocado slices and mix them together. Serve with a variety of crisp lettuce leaves and wholemeal bread and butter.

Guacamole

This spicy, creamed sauce from Mexico can be used as a dip with vegetable crudités, bread sticks, or *tortillas*, when served as a starter. It is also a useful sauce for cold chicken and fish. It can be made in three minutes in a food processor. It keeps overnight in the fridge if covered with cling-film.

Serves 2:

1 small avocado (peeled, stoned and roughly chopped)
1 dsrtsp finely chopped onion or 1 spring onion
1 small tomato (peeled, de-seeded)
½ fresh green chilli (seeded and chopped)
1 small clove garlic (peeled, crushed and chopped)
1 tbsp chopped fresh parsley or coriander leaves
salt, pepper, lemon juice and sugar (to taste)

Serves 6:

2 large avocados (peeled, stoned and roughly chopped)
1 tbsp finely chopped onion or two scallions
2 medium tomatoes (peeled and de-seeded)
1½ fresh green chillies (seeded and chopped)
1 large clove garlic (peeled, crushed and chopped)
2 tbsp fresh chopped parsley or coriander leaves
salt, pepper, lemon juice, sugar (to taste)

Place all the ingredients in the bowl of the food processor. Season lightly and process briefly. You do not want it to be too smooth. Check and adjust the seasoning.

Gazpacho

This cold tomato and garlic soup is one of the great Spanish peasant dishes. You will be served adulterated, watered-down, emasculated versions in restaurants but the real soup is hearty, rich and wonderful.

Serves 2:

2 slices of day-old, good home-made bread
250 ml cold water
1 tbsp wine vinegar
1 smallish clove garlic (peeled, crushed)
7 cm piece of cucumber
350 g ripe tomatoes
½ green pepper
½ onion (peeled, chopped)
1 tbsp olive oil
125 ml tomato juice
salt and freshly ground black pepper (to taste)

Serves 6:

5 slices of day-old, good home-made bread
600 ml cold water
2-3 tbsp wine vinegar (to taste)
2 large cloves garlic (peeled, crushed)
16 cm piece cucumber
1 kilo ripe tomatoes
2 green peppers
1 large Spanish onion (peeled, chopped)
3 tbsp olive oil
300 ml tomato juice
salt and freshly ground black pepper (to taste)

Put the bread to soak in 2 or 3 tablespoons of the cold water, all of the vinegar and the peeled and well-crushed garlic. Peel and then chop the cucumber in 1 cm pieces. Skin the tomatoes by placing them in a small bowl and pouring boiling water over them to cover. Count to thirty. The skin will split and is then easily peeled off. Cut the tomatoes in half and remove the seeds. (I never do either of these things but guests have a habit of not liking tomato skins and seeds.) Chop the flesh of the tomatoes roughly. De-seed the green pepper and chop the flesh. Peel and chop the onion. Set aside a small quantity of the chopped vegetables to be used as a garnish.

Classically, the bread and the vegetables should now be pounded together in a large mortar but it is permissible to use the food processor. Put the soaked bread, the garlic, the rest of the chopped vegetables, and the olive oil into the bowl of the processor. Process until they are well blended but not completely puréed. Add the tomato juice and blend for a short time. Now add just enough of the remaining water to get the consistency of a thickish soup. Taste for seasoning and add salt if necessary. Place the soup in a bowl in the fridge for at least an hour. On no account put ice cubes into it! Serve chilled with a garnish of the reserved vegetables, some chopped hard-boiled egg, and tiny croutons of bread fried in olive oil.

Spicy Prawns

It is often possible to buy fresh peeled prawns in a good fishmongers. If you are using frozen prawns you must defrost them before use.

Serves 2:

150-175 g peeled prawns
1 large clove garlic (peeled, crushed and finely chopped)
1½ tbsp good olive oil
½ tsp paprika
½ tsp cumin
2 cm piece fresh ginger root (peeled and finely chopped)
½ fresh chilli (de-seeded, finely chopped)
1 tbsp fresh coriander leaves or parsley (chopped)

Serves 6:

450-500 g peeled prawns
3 cloves garlic (peeled, crushed and finely chopped)
3 tbsp good olive oil
1½ tsp paprika
1½ tsp cumin
6 cm piece fresh root ginger (peeled, finely chopped)
1½ fresh chillies (de-seeded, finely chopped)
3 tbsp fresh coriander leaves or parsley (finely chopped)

Heat the olive oil in a pan and fry the garlic, fresh ginger, fresh chili for 1 minute. Add the spices and stir for a few seconds. Add the prawns and cook until they are heated through. Add the chopped coriander leaves or parsley and stir. Cook for 1 more minute. Serve very hot.

Vegetables and Salads

Italian Stir-fried Broccoli or Cauliflower

Stir-frying vegetables is not an exclusively Chinese technique. It is common wherever good fresh vegetables are valued. Many Italian stir-fried vegetable recipes call for the vegetables to be blanched first in boiling water then cooled rapidly in cold water. There is a minimal loss of vitamins and the green vegetables come up bright green and retain much of their texture and flavour.

Many people have difficulty cooking broccoli successfully. This is usually because they attempt to cook it until the stalk is tender, by which time the florets are hopelessly overcooked and falling off. There are three ways round this problem. The first requires you to divide the large heads into florets, no larger than your thumb, using a very sharp knife. Cut off the stalk close to the florets. Peel the skin from the stalks and slice them into thin rounds about 1 cm thick. These are put into the boiling water before the florets, which are kept back until the stalk is tender. The second method is to peel the stalks without separating them from their heads and then split them into four, stopping before you reach the head. They then cook almost as quickly as the florets. The third way is to reserve the stalks for another time and a recipe which allows a longer cooking-time. They can be peeled and split and used in any recipe which calls for leaf beet or even asparagus. They have a lot of flavour and should not be discarded.

Serves 2:

250 g broccoli (prepared as above)
1 clove garlic (peeled, crushed and finely chopped)
1½ tbsp olive oil
1 tbsp fresh chopped parsley

Serves 6:

1 kilo broccoli (prepared as above)
2-3 cloves garlic (peeled, crushed and finely chopped)
4 tbsp olive oil
3 tbsp fresh chopped parsley

Blanch the broccoli in rapidly boiling water for 3 minutes or until barely tender. Drain thoroughly. If you are not going to fry the broccoli at once, plunge it into cold water. When it is cool, drain it well. It will keep happily for a few hours without harming.

Heat the olive oil in a pan large enough to hold all of the broccoli in a single layer. Fry the garlic until it is just beginning to colour. Add the broccoli and the parsley and stir-fry for 2 minutes till just hot through. Sprinkle with a pinch of salt and serve at once.

Quick-fried Mange-tout

Serves 2:

200 g fresh mange-tout peas (or asparagus peas)
1 clove garlic (peeled, crushed and finely chopped)
2 tbsp *arachide* or sunflower oil
1 dsrtsp light soy sauce
1 dsrtsp chinese oyster sauce
1 tbsp stock
pinch of sugar

Serves 6 (or more when served with other Chinese dishes):

750 g fresh mange-tout
2 cloves garlic (peeled, crushed and finely chopped)
5 tbsp *arachide* or sunflower oil
1 tbsp light soy sauce
1 tbsp chinese oyster sauce
2 tbsp stock
good pinch of sugar

Top and tail the mange-tout. Heat a wok or large frying-pan until hot then add the oil. When the oil is very hot add the mange-tout and stir-fry over a high heat for 1 minute. Reduce the heat and fry the peas for another minute. Spoon out any excess oil which has not been taken up by the peas. Add the rest of the ingredients and cook over a medium heat for 2 minutes, stirring occasionally.

A variation is to omit the garlic, soy and oyster sauces but sprinkle 1-2 teaspoons sesame seeds over the peas just before serving.

Mushrooms with Garlic and Parsley

Serves 2:

250 g cultivated button mushrooms
1 small clove garlic (peeled, crushed and finely chopped)
2 tbsp olive oil
2 tbsp fresh chopped parsley
salt and freshly ground black pepper (to taste)

Serves 6:

750 g cultivated button mushrooms
2 small cloves garlic (peeled, crushed and finely chopped)
4 tbsp olive oil
3 tbsp fresh chopped parsley
salt and freshly ground black pepper (to taste)

This dish can be eaten hot as a vegetable or cold as a salad or as part of a mixed *hors d'oeuvres*.

Wipe the mushrooms clean with a damp cloth and slice thinly. Heat a large frying-pan over a medium heat and add the oil. Fry the garlic until it turns golden then turn up the heat and add the mushrooms. Cook until they have absorbed the oil. This will take only a few minutes. Turn the heat to low and cook until the juices begin to run from the mushrooms. This will happen quite quickly. Turn up the heat once more and stir-fry for 2-3 minutes. Don't be tempted to overcook them as they will become rubbery. Season, add the parsley. Serve hot or cold as required. A teaspoon of chopped fresh summer savory can be sprinkled over the mushrooms if you are serving them cold.

Italian Fried Potatoes

I have yet to find a potato dish (apart from frozen French fries) which can be prepared and cooked in fifteen minutes. Even small new potatoes can take that long. These twice-cooked potatoes come pretty close on the second cooking however and if you cook rather more boiled potatoes than you need one day, the next day you can have these ready in fifteen minutes flat. Alas, they cannot be frozen and don't keep for more than one day in the fridge. This is one of the reasons we eat rather more bread and pasta than potatoes on working days. These fried potatoes can be cooked in a frying-pan with olive oil (the best way) but are very successful and less trouble in a deep-fat fryer (as long as you change your oil regularly and don't fry fish in it).

Serves 2:

4 waxy potatoes boiled in their jackets
1 tbsp fresh chopped parsley
2 tbsp olive oil (if you're using a frying-pan)

Only use a waxy variety of potato as the floury ones disintegrate and make a mess of your deep-fat oil. Boil the four extra potatoes the day before and remove them from the pot when still slightly underdone. Peel off the skins as thinly as possible, removing any discoloured patches or eyes. Cut the potatoes into even-sized chunks if you are deep-frying them or into thick slices if frying them in a frying-pan.

In the frying-pan, heat the oil until just beginning to smoke; add the potatoes and cook until brown and crisp on all sides. Alternatively heat the oil in your deep-fat fryer to 170°C and fry the potatoes until evenly brown all over. Drain the potatoes on kitchen paper and serve at once sprinkled with the parsley and salt.

This dish is not suitable for serving to large numbers except as a garnish. You would have to cook the potatoes in batches and by the time the second and third batches are ready the first ones will have become soggy.

French Beans or Runner Beans with Spring Onion and Sesame Seeds

Serves 2:

200 g beans
15 g butter
2 spring onions (scallions)
1 dsrtsp sesame seeds
salt and freshly ground black pepper (to taste)

Serves 6:

750 g beans
50 g butter
6 spring onions (scallions)
1 tbsp sesame seeds
salt and freshly ground black pepper (to taste)

Top and tail the beans, removing any strings if necessary. Always buy French beans when they are young and narrow, no wider than a pencil. Runner beans can grow larger without becoming too tough but avoid the monster varieties which look as though they contain large seeds inside.

Bring a pot of salted water to the boil and drop in the beans. Cook them for 3-5 minutes, depending upon thickness. Beans should always have a distinct bite to them when eaten. Cook them too long and they lose their bright green colour. Drain them well and stir-fry the beans for 2 minutes in a frying-pan in which you have tossed the chopped spring onions and sesame seeds in the hot butter for one minute. Season with salt and pepper and serve sprinkled with fresh chopped summer savory.

French or Runner Bean Salad

If you omit the sesame seeds and use olive oil instead of butter then you can make a salad from the beans. Cook the beans as above but toss the spring onion in olive oil rather than butter. When the beans have been cooked in the hot oil with the onions for 2 minutes, quickly stir in a dessertspoonful of wine vinegar. You are, in effect, dressing the beans in a vinaigrette dressing. While these can be served hot, they are better kept overnight in the fridge and served cold the following day. Check the seasoning as cold dishes require more than hot.

Green Salad

Strictly speaking, a green salad should be exactly what the name implies—a dish of green leaves dressed simply with good oil and wine vinegar and a little seasoning. If you stick to supermarket butterhead lettuce then it is the most unappetising salad I know.

There are many much more interesting and flavoursome leaves available in specialist vegetable shops—crisp cos, endives, iceberg, rocket, lamb's lettuce; the chicories; and, to stretch a point, all the various red-leaved varieties: radiccio, lollo rosa, red oak leaf; the peppery cresses which can be added in smaller quantities; and then there are the other leaves from the garden: spinach, nasturtium, dandelion, sorrel, beetroot; finally all the different herbs and their flowers. Seasonal changes can be rung on the basic green salad through the whole year.

Always separate the leaves from the stalk with your fingers and wash the leaves in cold running water. Dry them thoroughly with kitchen paper or a clean tea-towel.

The salad dressing should be a simple mixture of good,

first pressing, virgin, olive oil with the best wine vinegar you can afford. I use a thick, fruity green oil from Greek kalamata olives. Season sparingly with minimal salt and a little freshly ground black pepper, perhaps with the addition of a tiny amount of French mustard, a tiny amount of crushed clove of garlic. The leaves should just be coated in dressing, not swimming in a puddle of it in the bottom of the bowl. Two tablespoonsful will dress a generous salad for two people.

When to serve the salad can be argued about. The French serve it after the main course to clear the palate before the cheese; Americans often serve it at the beginning of a meal; Italians serve it with the secondo, the second course of meat or fish after the pasta. We seem to have acquired the habit of serving it with the main course as an alternative to hot vegetables. Purists, especially the French, tell you not to drink wine with the salad as the wine will be ruined by the vinegar in the dressing. I suppose they have a point but one might argue with equal justification, that some of the wines they send us will not taste as good as a good French or Italian wine vinegar.

Main Courses in Fifteen Minutes

Chicken Breasts in Butter and Lemon

Serves 2:

2 chicken breast fillets (skin removed)
juice of ½ lemon
30 g butter
1 tbsp olive oil or vegetable oil
a handful of chopped fresh parsley
salt and freshly ground black pepper (to taste)

Serves 6:

6 chicken breast fillets (skinned)
juice of 1 large lemon
70 g butter
2 tbsp olive oil or vegetable oil
3 handfuls of chopped fresh parsley
salt and freshly ground black pepper (to taste)

When you buy a chicken breast fillet off the bone, it is divided naturally into two unequal-sized muscles, the smaller loosely attached to the under side of the large one. Separate them with your fingers. You must now divide the larger muscle into two. To do this place it on a chopping board (skin side out) and place your left hand (if you are right-handed) flat on top of it and press it down lightly. With a very sharp chef's knife slice the chicken horizontally into two equal pieces. Each breast is now divided into three pieces of more or less equal thickness which will cook evenly.

Heat the oil and half of the butter in a heavy-bottomed frying-pan over a medium heat. When the fat is hot but not burning, fry the chicken pieces to brown and seal them on both sides. This will take a minute for each side. Even with the present fears of salmonella be careful not to overcook them or they will become leathery and tough. The juices should run clear. Remove the chicken pieces to a hot plate and keep them warm. Season them with the salt and pepper. Add the lemon juice to the pan along with 2 tablespoons of water and deglaze it by scraping loose any residues with a spatula. Add the rest of the butter and the chopped parsley and, lowering the heat slightly, mix the contents of the pan thoroughly. Return the chicken pieces to the pan and cook for another 2 minutes. Serve at once. Veal escalopes can be cooked using this method as long as they are lightly coated in plain flour just before frying. Like the chicken, it is important not to overcook them as they, too, can become tough.

Escalope of Veal with Marsala

Serves 2:

2 veal escalopes (each 100 g and roughly ½ cm thick)
2 tbsp plain flour
4 tbsp Marsala (Italian fortified wine)
1 tbsp olive oil or vegetable oil
45 g butter

This is not a dish I would recommend you to cook for more than two or three people unless you have help in the kitchen. It requires a lot of last-minute attention and three heavy frying-pans on the go at the same time. However, these are the quantities.

Serves 6:

6 veal escalopes (each 100 g and roughly ½ cm thick)
5 tbsp plain flour
9 tbsp Marsala
3 tbsp olive oil or vegetable oil
100 g butter (cut into small cubes)

Heat the oil over a medium heat in a heavy-bottomed pan (two or three pans if you are attempting to cook this for six people). Just before you add them to the pan coat each escalope in plain flour. Shake off any excess flour. Brown each escalope on both sides. (Rather less than 1 minute per side if the oil is hot enough.) Remove the escalopes as they are done, season them, and keep them warm. Remove all but a tablespoonful of oil from the pan. Deglaze the pan with the Marsala, add the butter and when the sauce thickens return the escalopes to the pan with any juices which may have run from the meat. Turn the escalopes over in the sauce a couple of times and serve at once.

Chicken Livers with Sage and Onion

We all need to eat liver regularly to maintain a healthy, balanced diet. This dish is quick, highly nutritious and very tasty.

Serves 2:

200 g chicken livers
1 small onion (peeled and very finely chopped)
20 g butter
4-6 fresh sage leaves (depending on size)
2 tbsp dry white wine or dry sherry
salt and pepper (to taste)

Serves 6:

600 g chicken livers
1 large onion (peeled and very finely chopped)
60 g butter
8-10 sage leaves (depending on size)
6 tbsp dry white wine or dry sherry
salt and pepper (to taste)

Wash the livers in cold water, trim them of any fat and green spots, remove the hearts (if any). Dry them well on kitchen paper. In a heavy-bottomed frying-pan large enough to hold all the livers without crowding, melt the butter over a medium heat and cook the onion until translucent but not browned. Raise the heat to high and add the sage leaves and the livers. You can finely shred the sage leaves if you like but it is not absolutely necessary. Stir-fry the livers until they have firmed and are cooked but not dried out. They should retain a moist pinkness. Remove the livers onto a hot plate and keep them warm. Deglaze the pan with the wine. When the sauce has thickened return the livers to the pan and stir them in the sauce to coat them. Serve when the livers are very hot.

Trout or Bream Baked in Paper

Fish is one of the best fast foods and few of us eat it in sufficient quantity for our health and well-being. This is just about the simplest way of cooking fish I know. It also preserves all of its natural goodness. Served with some good home-made bread and a salad, it is a completely balanced meal. This dish has another advantage in that it is so simple that it hardly requires your presence in the kitchen if you have guests.

Serves 2:

2 whole trout or bream (about 200 g each)
1 tbsp fresh chopped herbs (3 different from thyme, rosemary, parsley, basil, marjoram or fennel leaves)
1 small clove garlic (peeled and crushed)
1 tbsp lemon juice
1½ tbsp olive oil
salt and freshly ground black pepper (to taste)

Serves 6:

6 whole trout or bream (about 200 g each)
3 tbsp herbs (mixture as above)
1 large clove garlic (peeled and crushed)
juice of ½ lemon
4½ tbsp olive oil
salt and freshly ground black pepper (to taste)

Cut squares of greaseproof paper large enough to fold up into parcels round each fish with a tuck at each end and a fold-over on top. The fishes should be gutted and de-scaled. Leave the heads on the fishes as this holds them together and traps the stuffing while it is cooking.

Finely chop all the herbs and peel and crush the garlic. Put them into a bowl with the oil, lemon juice and seasoning. Let them stand in the bowl for at least 15 minutes for the flavours to mingle. Lay each fish in turn on its wrapping paper and spoon a little of the herb mixture into the cavity. Fold up the paper to form a neat even-sized parcel round each fish in turn. Place the parcels in a single layer on a baking tray or dish. Cook in a preheated oven for 15 minutes at 200°C (400°F, gas mark 6).

To serve, transfer each parcel to a hot plate, snip off the ends and open out the top fold. It is customary to serve the fish on the paper to retain all the juices.

Scallop, Prawn and Vegetable Kebab

Serves 2:

3-5 scallops (depending upon size)
6 large prawns (Dublin Bay) in the shell
100 ml white wine
1 tbsp olive oil
1 tbsp fresh chopped tarragon and parsley, thyme or marjoram
30 g melted butter
4 lemon wedges
4 cherry tomatoes
1 small onion (peeled and divided into quarters)
flesh of 1 small red or green pepper cut into squares
salt, freshly ground black pepper and a pinch of paprika

Serves 6:

6-9 scallops (depending on size)
18 large prawns (Dublin Bay) in the shell
300 ml white wine
3 tbsp olive oil
3-4 tbsp fresh chopped mixed herbs (including tarragon)
100 g melted butter
12 lemon wedges
12 cherry tomatoes
3 small onions (peeled and divided into quarters)
flesh of 2 red or green peppers cut into squares
salt, freshly ground black pepper, three pinches paprika

Mix the wine, oil and herbs in a bowl. Remove the scallops from their shells and discard the small crescent-shaped muscle. If they are large cut them in two and put into the marinade. Remove the prawns' heads and claws by twisting them off. With a very sharp knife score the inside surface of the tail shell and force the shell apart to remove the flesh from the tail. Place the tail shell along with the prawn tails in the marinade. You must leave the shellfish in the marinade for at least half an hour and if possible for as long as 4 hours.

Prepare the lemons, onions, tomatoes and sweet peppers. Preheat the grill while you thread alternate pieces of vegetable and shellfish onto thin metal skewers. Brush with the melted butter and season with pepper and paprika. Place the skewers under the grill and cook for 6-8 minutes, turning frequently and brushing with melted butter as necessary. The shellfish should be opaque and firm to the touch. Serve hot with pitta breads and salad.

Italian Flat Omelettes

Omelettes of any kind are quick and convenient but the

Italians have a method which appeals to me very much and has become the firm favourite in our household. They take longer to cook, are much more substantial, and benefit from what we call *planned obsolescence.* (I know that's not a correct term but it is, nevertheless, what this sort of pre-planning has come to be called in our family.)

If, as a working person who cooks, you can master this simple concept you will gain a reputation for inventiveness and mastery which far outstrips the truth. It means that you cook sufficient quantities of certain vegetables or fish or even meats to ensure that you have leftovers. Thought out carefully in advance, this can mean that you have the makings of another dish tomorrow and part of the preparation done for a third. For instance, many dishes call for chopped onion which has been fried until soft and browned. So, with *planned obsolescence*, you cook more than you need for the dish at hand, but enough to have onions for the flat Italian omelette you intend to cook tomorrow. You will have saved yourself twenty minutes.

Serves 2:

3 small eggs
3 tbsp olive oil
200 g onions (preferably red ones, peeled and finely sliced)
30 g freshly grated Parmesan or another grana-type cheese
30 g butter
1 tsp freshly chopped marjoram
salt and freshly ground black pepper (to taste)

Serves 6:

6 large eggs
500 g onions (red, peeled and finely sliced)

70 g freshly grated grana-type cheese
50 g butter
2 tsp freshly chopped marjoram
salt and freshly ground black pepper (to taste)

Prepare the onions by frying them gently until soft and just brown in a little olive oil. (See what I mean about *planned obsolescence*?) Beat the eggs in a bowl and incorporate the onions, the cheese, the herbs and seasoning.

Melt the butter in the pan (you will need a very large one if you are cooking this for six people) and allow it to foam. Pour the egg mixture into the pan. Turn the heat down as low as you can and cook at this setting for 14-15 minutes until the eggs are set and thick. Only the top of the omelette should remain soft and runny. Now put the pan under a hot grill for 1-2 minutes, moving its position if necessary to brown and set the top of the omelette. Serve the omelette like a pie, cut into triangular wedges. Italian fried potatoes go well with this but better still is focaccia bread.

There are several different variations which can be worked with this basic recipe.

If you cut a potato (or three) into a 1 cm dice and pan-fry it in olive oil until really crisp you can add it to the eggs just after you put them in the pan. You can omit the onions and add two heaped tablespoons of fresh chopped herbs. Fresh mint and parsley is a good mixture.

If you can get any Italian bacon, *pancetta*, chop about 60 g (or 180 g) into a small dice and fry it until it is crisp. Add this to the omelette when it is in the pan.

Soufflé Omelette

Often served as sweet omelettes with fruit or jam fillings, I prefer these fluffy omelettes as a savoury. My favourite filling is simple tomato and basil. Unless you are prepared to have more than one pan on the go these are not really suitable for serving to more than two people.

Serves 2:

- 4 eggs
- 2-3 tomatoes
- 2 tsp basil (fresh for preference, if not just ½ tsp dried)
- 20 g butter
- salt and freshly ground black pepper (to taste)

Skin the tomatoes by pouring boiling water over them to loosen the skins. Halve the tomatoes and remove the core and seeds. Chop the flesh roughly and sprinkle the fresh basil over it.

Separate the yolks from the egg whites. Beat the yolks with a little salt. Put the whites in a separate bowl and whisk them until they are stiff. Fold one-quarter of the beaten egg white into the yolks and then fold this mixture into the whites. Do this gently to prevent the whites collapsing.

Heat the butter in an omelette pan until it foams. Pour in the egg mixture and cook over a low heat without stirring. Spread the tomato and basil over the surface of the omelette. Season. The eggs will puff up and gradually become almost set in the centre. Slip the pan under a hot grill to finish cooking the top. Don't overcook; it should still be slightly creamy in the centre of the omelette. Serve at once.

Fast Puddings

Watermelon with Lemon Juice

Remove the flesh from two (or six) single serving sized wedges of watermelon. Cut the flesh up into bite-sized chunks and put them into a bowl. Pour lemon juice over the melon and put it into the fridge until you have had your main course. So simple and refreshing.

Freezer Fruit Salad

If you have a microwave oven and freeze bags of soft fruits in your deep-freeze when they are in season, you can put up this pudding in seconds.

If you freeze fruits like this they should always be frozen on trays, separated from leaves, stalks and each other until the individual fruits are completely frozen. They can then be bagged into suitable amounts and take up much less room. Some frozen packs of fruit which you can buy are all stuck together and it is difficult to separate a small amount. Choose three fruits from the following: blackcurrants, stoned black cherries, redcurrants, raspberries, loganberries, dessert gooseberries, whortleberries (fraughans).

Serves 2:

250 g mixed frozen fruit
3 tbsp Grenadine or blackcurrant syrup

Serves 6:

750 g frozen fruit
8 tbsp Grenadine or blackcurrant syrup

Put the fruits (with the exception of raspberries or loganberries if you have chosen them) into a bowl and cover them with the Grenadine. Cover the bowl with cling-film and pierce two holes in it. Thaw the fruit in the microwave for 10 minutes, stirring twice in this time. Now add the raspberries or loganberries and allow the mixture to stand for half an hour until they have thawed.

Strawberries with Curd Cheese

This is a traditional dish in both France and Ireland and makes a delightful change from strawberries and cream.

Serves 2:

100 g fresh strawberries
150 g smooth curd cheese
50 ml fresh cream
sugar (optional) to taste
fresh borage flowers (if available)

Serves 6:

300 g fresh strawberries
450 g smooth curd cheese
150 ml fresh cream
sugar (optional) to taste
fresh borage flowers (if available)

Hull the strawberries. Whisk the cream and the cheese together. Slice the strawberries. Spoon the cream cheese mixture onto one side of the plate and the strawberries onto the other. Decorate the cheese mixture with the borage flowers and a couple of small borage leaves. (Both are edible.) You can sprinkle sugar over the strawberries if you wish but I think it spoils the slightly sharp taste of the pudding.

7
Loving Care for Two

Starters

Mixed Deep-fried Vegetables

Serves 2:

for the batter:

8 tbsp warm water
40 g plain flour
30 g grated Parmesan (or other grana-type cheese)
1 egg

vegetables:

300-400g lightly cooked mixed vegetables (cauliflower, broccoli, sliced courgette, carrots, mushrooms)
2 lemon wedges
salt and freshly ground black pepper (to taste)

Prepare the vegetables by dividing them into small florets (cauliflower and broccoli), slicing the courgettes and carrots into ½ cm rounds, dividing button mushrooms in two. Cook the vegetables (except the mushrooms) in 1 pint of rapidly boiling salted water for 2-3 minutes until barely tender. Keep this stock for later use as a basic vegetable stock.

Make a batter with the water, flour, cheese and egg and season it. If you have a food processor use it. Put some oil in a wide pan (it should be 1 cm deep). Heat the oil until a drop of the batter sets immediately it is added to the oil. Dip the vegetables (including the mushrooms) into the batter and fry them until golden-brown all over. If you are doing them in batches keep them warm on kitchen paper until all are cooked. Serve at once with lemon wedges.

This can be served as a starter or as an accompaniment to a main course. It is impossible to prepare for large numbers of people unless you have a commercial-sized deep-fryer.

Cheese Fondue

This is a flexible dish. In small quantities it makes a pleasant starter; made in larger amounts, served with good bread and a substantial salad, it makes a successful main meal and it can be served as part of a buffet. We often eat it as a family supper on Sunday, the only day we cook a large luncheon.

There are many cheeses which respond well to this method of cooking but they are all of the hard or semi-hard types. You can always add a small quantity of a soft type but they should never be made the basis of the dish. Do not be tempted to look upon this dish as a dustbin for all the dried-out lumps of cheese in the fridge, however, as a mixture of cheeses does not always turn out to have the taste you expected.

Cheeses I have found successful as bases for this dish (usually mixed with just one other from the list) are: Swiss Emmenthal and Gruyère, obviously, Scotch Dunlop, mature cheddar types, Lancashire, Irish Blarney and Dutch Edam, Red Leicester. I often add a quantity of one of the hard grana cheeses like Parmesan, but this is a waste. However, if you use the Irish Regato cheese which is widely available and much cheaper (but extremely good), it is not quite so extravagant.

Serves 2:

2 cups (lightly filled, not pressed down) grated cheese
1 small clove garlic (peeled and crushed)
2 tbsp fruit chutney
2-3 tbsp dry white wine (or Chinese rice wine)
2 tsp very finely chopped fresh parsley
home made, crusty bread cut into 1 inch cubes

Serves 6 (or more):

This is one of the very few recipes where you simply multiply all the ingredients to suit your numbers.

Grate the cheese either by hand or in the food processor with a suitable grating disc installed. Do not be tempted to crumble it with the standard blade as this always has an adverse effect on the way the cheese melts, making separation likely. Peel and crush the garlic and chop it very finely.

Put all the ingredients into a heavy-bottomed saucepan or the pan of a fondue set if you have one. Place this over the lowest possible heat. If you try and hurry this melting stage you will end up with a separated, gluey mess. This is far more likely to happen if you use a "factory" cheese—the ubiquitous shrink-wrapped slabs. You'd need a degree in food science to work out why this should be so. It is possible to use this as long as you have a good proportion of "real" cheese in the pot with it. If you are melting the cheese on a gas ring then it is a good idea to use a wok cradle to lift the pot further away from the flame. The methylated spirit burners of most fondue sets work as long as you have the flame set to its lowest until all the cheese has melted. Stir it gently once or twice while the cheese is melting.

The better the bread you serve with this the better it tastes. Drink the rest of the wine with it.

Dressed Crab

Crabs demand a certain devotion to the pleasures of the table—which is why fishmongers can charge a king's ransom for the dressed crabs sitting there in state with the claw and body meat arranged in stripes in the classic French manner. I have two objections to this: I hate paying up to six times more than I need for anything; I like the claw meat and the body meat mixed because the texture is better.

Bought crab meat, at even greater cost than whole dressed crab, usually contains only the claw meat. While this is useful for some dishes it has rather less than half of the real taste of crab. Crab sticks, so-called, are an abomination, often concocted from unclassified fish meat with added "crab flavouring." I always buy my crabs at the local harbour. They are always alive, kept in boxes underwater and hauled up for you to inspect. Watch out! They have a tendency to lie "doggo" and are not averse to taking a nasty nip out of anyone who pokes them unwarily. I once bought six crabs but had to pay for seven. One of them grabbed my finger and by the time I got away he had scuttled back to the safety of the harbour. You will need a strong bag or box in which to transport them home. I use an old heavy plastic coal bag kept for the purpose. Tie the top firmly with string. Crabs are very difficult to catch in the depths of a car boot.

Place the crabs in a large pot of heavily salted warm water with a heavy lid. Bring this to the boil. The crabs faint from the heat and don't feel a thing. I tell myself this. When it boils turn down the heat and simmer them for 20 minutes. Pour off the water and allow the crabs to drain, the right way up.

Twist the claws from the body and crack them open, section by section, with a sharp tap of a heavy hammer. Extract all the meat using a skewer for the knacky bits. It sounds more difficult than it actually is. Be careful to pick out any shell fragments and the clear, stiff central membrane. Pull out the central plate underneath the shell to which all the legs were attached. Discard the grey gills (or dead man's fingers) and the stomach sac. Scoop out all the brown meat from the shell and any adhering to the body. A good-sized crab will yield 150-200 g of meat—more than enough for two as a starter.

Crab Mayonnaise

Serves 2:

150-200 g crab meat (white and brown mixed)
4 tbsp mayonnaise
1 spring onion (scallion) chopped or 1 tbsp chopped chives
Wholemeal bread and butter

Mix the mayonnaise and the crab meat together and garnish with the chopped onion or chives. Season to taste and eat with wholemeal bread and butter and a green salad.

Serves 6:

Treble all the ingredients.

Crab with Garlic Butter

Serves 2:

150-200 g crab meat (mixed white and brown or separate)

1 clove garlic (peeled, crushed and finely chopped)
60 g butter
4 tbsp fresh chopped parsley
salt and freshly ground black pepper (to taste)

Put the crab meat into small ramekins or serving dishes. Melt the butter and add the very finely chopped garlic and the parsley. Season and pour over the crab. Serve at once with wholemeal bread and butter.

Oysters
It is difficult today to believe that oysters were once considered the food of the common poor and that servants used to complain when they got too many of them. Nowadays they are an expensive delight. They require no cooking, virtually no preparation and eating them at home is now the least expensive way of eating them.

Oysters are graded by size on a downward scale of 1-4. Sold by the dozen, six is really the minimum individual serving. Oysters can be cooked very briefly in some recipes but overcooking makes them tough and rubbery.

The shells should be firmly closed when you buy them. Rinse the shells under cold, running water, scrubbing them if necessary. Cover your holding hand with a thick glove or cloth. Using a short-bladed oyster knife, insert the point of the blade next to the hinge of the shell. Work it in. Twist to prise open the shell. Separate the flesh from the shell with the blade, discard the lid of the shell and serve the oysters on the other half-shell. Serve with good wholemeal bread and butter, a wedge of lemon, and a tiny splash of tabasco if that is to your taste. The traditional accompaniment is stout or champagne. The common poor, how are you!

Broad Beans with Bacon and Cream
This is the way to make older, larger broad beans (the sort

that reach the shops and get frozen) as good to eat as tender young beans straight from the garden. It has been relegated to this chapter because of the time it takes to prepare them but, if you are prepared to put in the time they can be prepared in larger quantities.

Serves 2:

500 g broad beans
60 g *pancetta* (or unsmoked streaky bacon)
15 g butter
2 tbsp fresh cream
1 tbsp fresh chopped chives or summer savory
freshly ground black pepper to taste

Dice the *pancetta* or streaky bacon very finely and fry it in a little of the butter until it is really crisp.

Remove the bacon from the pan and set it to drain on kitchen paper. Remove the beans from their pods and boil for 3-8 minutes in rapidly boiling salted water until they are tender. Test them after 3 minutes. When they are tender but not mushy, drain them, cool them, and slip off the outer skin of each bean. This is quite easy, a gentle squeeze is all that is necessary. Add the rest of the butter to the pan in which the bacon was fried and when it is hot but not burning add the beans and stir-fry them for 1 minute. Season with black pepper and add the cream. Cook, stirring until the beans are piping hot. Serve the beans in a hot dish with the crisp bacon pieces and the summer savory sprinkled over them.

I like to eat broad beans with fish and this recipe is good with grilled, steamed or microwaved fish of all kinds. They also make an unusual and tasty filling for an omelette.

Vegetables and Salads

Cauliflower Cheese

Much tastier than the usual cauliflower dosed in a white cheese sauce and less trouble to prepare.

Serves 2:

500 g cauliflower (roughly ½ medium-sized head)
20 g butter
20 g grated hard grana cheese (Irish Regato)
salt and freshly ground black pepper (to taste)

Separate the cauliflower into small florets and cook in rapidly boiling water until barely tender. Drain well. (This part can be done several hours in advance.)

Grate the cheese and butter a baking dish just large enough to hold the cauliflower in one layer. Lay out the cauliflower in the dish and season it. (Purists would use white pepper for cauliflower.) Sprinkle the cheese over the cauliflower and dot with a little butter. Bake for about 15 minutes at 200°C (425°F, gas mark 6). The cheese will form a light, crisp, golden-brown crust.

French Beans with Onion and Tomato

Another of those flexible dishes suitable as either a starter or as an accompaniment to a main course. A little fiddly to prepare but well worth the effort.

Serves 2:

300 g French beans
1 small onion (peeled and very finely sliced)
30 g butter or 2 tbsp olive oil
2 tbsp chopped tinned tomatoes
½ tsp fresh oregano or marjoram

1 tbsp fresh chopped parsley
salt and freshly ground black pepper (to taste)

Serves 6:

1 kilo French beans
1 large onion (peeled and very finely sliced)
50 g butter or 3-4 tbsp olive oil
6 tbsp chopped tinned tomatoes
2 tsp fresh oregano or marjoram
2 tbsp fresh chopped parsley
salt and freshly ground black pepper (to taste)

Top and tail the beans. Blanch them in boiling salted water until barely tender. In a wide pan melt the butter or heat the oil and stew the onions until very soft and golden but not brown. Drain the tomato, chop it and mix with the fresh marjoram or oregano and in a small pan stir-fry it with a little butter or oil from the onions until the excess liquid evaporates. Add the beans to the pan with the onions and stir-fry them until heated through. Add the tomato mixture, season and fry for another minute, stirring all the time to coat the beans with the sauce. Serve hot. The beans should still be crisp.

Meat and Fish Dishes

Pork Chops with Apple and Mustard Sauce

Serves 2:

2 pork loin chops
10 g butter
2 large apples (firm apples that will not disintegrate)
2 tbsp dry white wine or cider
100 ml cream

2-2½ tbsp Dijon mustard
salt and freshly ground black pepper (to taste)

Serves 6:

6 pork loin chops
20 g butter
6 large apples
6 tbsp white wine
250 ml cream
6 tbsp Dijon mustard
salt and freshly ground black pepper to taste

Peel, core and thinly slice the apples (into rounds.) Butter a baking dish large enough to take the chops in a single layer. Spread the apples in this dish and bake in a preheated oven for 15 minutes at 200°C (425°F, gas mark 6). While the apples are baking, brown the chops on both sides in a pan over a medium heat. Place them on top of the apples in the baking dish. Deglaze the pan with the wine or cider and pour this sauce over the chops. Mix the cream and mustard to your taste, season the chops and pour the creamed mustard over the chops. Shake the dish so that the sauce gets down to the apples as well. Bake for a further 15 minutes.

This sauce begs to have really good home-made bread dunked in it and although it is a French recipe, Italian focaccia is perfect for this. The focaccia will cook quite happily on the top shelf of the oven while the apples and chops bake on the middle shelf.

Veal Chops with Garlic, Rosemary and Breadcrumbs
Veal chops are not as expensive as escalopes. Serve this dish with a moist vegetable dish. Once again this dish is difficult to prepare for more than four people unless you have a very large kitchen and another pair of hands. For

four, use two pans and double the ingredients except for the oil. (3 tablespoons would be plenty.)

Serves 2:

2 veal chops (about 1 cm thick)
1 egg
2 tsp fresh rosemary (finely chopped)
70 g plain dry breadcrumbs
2 tbsp olive oil
20 g butter
2 cloves garlic (peeled and crushed)
2 lemon wedges
salt and freshly ground black pepper (to taste)

Lay out three plates, one for the breadcrumbs, one for the beaten egg and one to take the crumbed chops. Knock out the corner bone of the chop or remove it with a sharp knife. Flatten the chops between sheets of greaseproof paper with the flat of a cleaver. Dip the chops into the egg and the breadcrumbs. Sprinkle each chop with the rosemary and press it firmly into the crumbs.

Put the oil, butter and the crushed garlic into a frying-pan wide enough to take both chops side by side. Heat until the butter begins to foam. Fry the chops on each side in turn until the breadcrumbs form a light brown crust. Remove the garlic from the pan when one side of the chops is done. It has done its job of flavouring the oil but will turn bitter if fried too long.

Drain the chops on kitchen paper before serving very hot with the lemon wedges. Accompany with the French bean recipe from this chapter or with fried sweet peppers.

Lamb Chops with Crisp Cheese and Breadcrumbs

Best made with tender spring lamb. Buy side loin chops or centre loin with any little bones removed and excess fat trimmed away or not (as you like—there will be very little).

Serves 2:

2 lamb chops
2 tbsp grated Parmesan or Irish Regato cheese
40 g dried breadcrumbs
1 small beaten egg
1 tsp fresh chopped thyme
salt and freshly ground black pepper (to taste)
good pinch of paprika
vegetable oil for frying

Serves 6:

6 lamb chops
6 tbsp grated grana-type cheese
120 g dried breadcrumbs
2 large beaten eggs
salt and freshly ground black pepper (to taste)
two good pinches paprika
3 tsp fresh chopped thyme
vegetable oil for frying

This is very like the last recipe in method. It poses the same problems when cooking for more than four people.

Mix the breadcrumbs, the grated cheese, paprika, salt, pepper and thyme together thoroughly. (Shaking them up together in a plastic bag is one reliable way.) Lay out three plates, one for the beaten egg, one for the breadcrumb mixture, and one to take the crumbed chops. Flatten the chops with the flat of a cleaver as before and egg and then breadcrumb them. They can be prepared ahead to this point and stored in the fridge.

Heat the oil in the pan until really hot and then cook the chops on both sides until they have a really nice brown crust. They will take about 4-6 minutes to cook.

The meat should still be slightly pink and juicy when cut. Drain on kitchen paper and serve piping hot.

Minute Steak with Tomato and Mushroom Sauce
This recipe is only as good as the steak that goes into it. In my experience not all minute steaks sold by some butchers qualify. Realistically (taking cost into account), thin slices of topside or ball of the round (both sections of the larger joint of round steak) are suitable if the beast has been well hung. If you are doubtful about the tenderness of your steaks, a few hours in a marinade will help tenderise them.

Serves 2:

180-200 g meat in two even slices
3 tbsp olive oil
60 g button mushrooms (cleaned and sliced)
1 medium onion (peeled and finely sliced)
30 g plain flour
4 tbsp red wine
2 tbsp chopped tinned tomatoes (Italian plum)
2 tsp fresh chopped marjoram or oregano (½ tsp dried)
salt and freshly ground black pepper (to taste)

Serves 6:

500-550 g meat cut in six even slices
6 tbsp olive oil
200 g mushrooms (cleaned and sliced)
2 medium onions (peeled and finely sliced)
100 g plain flour
200 ml red wine
1 tin Italian plum tomatoes (chopped)
4 tsp fresh oregano or marjoram (finely chopped)
salt and freshly ground black pepper (to taste)

Heat half of the oil in a pan. Put in the tomatoes and stew until the excess liquid is driven off and the oil begins to separate from the tomato pulp. Heat the other half of the oil in a separate pan and fry the onions slowly until translucent and soft. Heat a wide frying-pan which will take the steaks in one layer. You will need two if cooking for six. Dip the steaks in seasoned flour just before you fry them on the pan using some of the oil from the onions. Shake off excess flour before putting them on the pan. Fry them briefly to brown and seal on both sides. Add the onions while they are on their second side. Take the steaks up and keep them warm. (Not too warm because you don't want them to keep cooking or they will get tough. Tip the mushrooms into the pan and stir-fry them for 2 minutes, then add the wine. Let the wine bubble and reduce, stirring and scraping the residue from the base of the pan. Add the tomato paste and stir well. Return the steaks to the pan and just let them warm through for a minute. Serve the steaks on a hot plate with the sauce spooned over them. Eat at once with good bread or Italian fried potatoes.

Rabbit Stew with Garlic

This is a Spanish dish which can be prepared using pieces of farmed rabbit (which are now widely available and extremely good value as well as being very tasty) for either two or six people.

Serves 2:

300-400 g rabbit (in two pieces)
2 tbsp plain flour
2 tbsp white wine vinegar
60 ml dry sherry or white wine
60 ml olive oil
4-6 cloves garlic (peeled, crushed and roughly chopped)
salt and freshly ground black pepper (to taste)

Serves 6:

1-1¼, kilo rabbit (in six pieces)
4 tbsp plain flour
4 tbsp white wine vinegar
175 ml dry sherry or white wine
120 ml olive oil
8-12 cloves garlic (peeled, crushed and roughly chopped)
salt and freshly ground black pepper (to taste)

Put the pieces of rabbit in a shallow dish and sprinkle them all over with the white wine vinegar. Let them marinate in the fridge overnight.

The next day, pat the pieces of rabbit dry with kitchen paper and roll them lightly in the flour which has been seasoned with salt and freshly ground black pepper. Heat the oil in a wide flat heavy-bottomed pan with a tightly fitting lid. Fry the rabbit pieces gently until the flour is golden on all sides. Add the garlic and allow it to fry gently for 2 minutes. Add the sherry or wine and allow it to bubble up to evaporate the alcohol. Cover tightly and stew the rabbit over a gentle heat for 40 minutes. The rabbit should be very tender and the liquid almost evaporated.

Serve with lots of good, fresh, home-made bread, two separate salads of sliced tomatoes and crisp green lettuce, and Italian twice-cooked potatoes.

Smoked Haddock Soufflé

Once you have the knack, soufflés are no trouble whether for two people or six. But they cannot be kept waiting, and there is no worse feeling than waiting for late arrivals while the soufflé goes from bad to totally collapsed. Reserve this dish for punctual people.

Serves 2:

125 ml béchamel sauce
2 egg yolks
3 egg whites
1 tbsp cream
180 g cooked, flaked, smoked haddock
salt and freshly ground black pepper (to taste)
butter to grease a 750 ml soufflé dish

Serves 6:

250 ml béchamel sauce
4 egg yolks
6 egg whites
3 tbsp cream
375 g cooked, flaked, smoked haddock
salt and freshly ground black pepper (to taste)
butter to grease a 1.5 litre soufflé dish

Prepare the béchamel sauce and allow it to cool a little before beating in the egg yolks, one at a time. Over a very gentle heat cook this mixture to make it thicken a little. Remove it from the heat again and add the fish and the cream. Preheat the oven to 175°C (350°F, gas mark 4). Butter the soufflé dish. Beat the egg whites using a hand-held electric whisk until they are stiff. Warm the fish mixture carefully until it is just hot to the touch and then fold this mixture into the egg whites. Be gentle. Pour the mixture, gently, into the buttered soufflé dish, smooth the top, run your thumb round the top of the dish, near the rim, to make a shallow groove in the mixture. (This, by some alchemy, causes the soufflé to have a raised high "cap" which is much treasured by soufflé *aficionados*.) Bake for 15-16 minutes, until puffed and just firm in the centre. Serve immediately.

Spinach Soufflé

This is a lovely vegetarian dish and is based on a creamy béchamel sauce. This is a common feature of many savory soufflés.

Serves 2:

300 g cooked puréed spinach
15 g butter
15 g flour
50 ml cream
1 large egg yolk
2 egg whites
a pinch of grated nutmeg
1 tsp grated Parmesan cheese
salt and freshly ground black pepper (to taste)

Serves 6:

900 g cooked, puréed spinach
45 g butter
45 g flour
150 ml cream
2 egg yolks
3 egg whites
good pinch grated nutmeg
2 tsp grated Parmesan cheese
salt and freshly ground black pepper (to taste)

Wash, cook, drain and squeeze the spinach until all the water is removed from the leaves. Purée in the food processor or mouli-sieve. Make a béchamel sauce with the butter, flour and cream and season it with the nutmeg, cheese, salt and pepper. Add the puréed spinach and mix thoroughly. Add the egg yolk. Cool.

Whisk the egg whites until stiff. Add about one-quarter of the whites to the béchamel mixture to lighten it and then gently fold the mixture into the rest of the egg whites. Half fill individual ramekins with the mixture, sprinkling a little cheese over the surface. Bake in a preheated oven for 10-15 minutes (depending on the size of the dishes) at 200°C (425°F, gas mark 6). Serve at once.

Marinated Grilled Chicken with Lemon

If you ever get your hands on true free-range chicken, this is the way to cook it. It works with intensively reared fowl but does not remove the taste of the fish-meal they have been fed.

Serves 2:

1 whole small chicken (1 kilo)
juice of 1 lemon
2 tbsp olive oil
salt to taste
1 tbsp freshly ground black pepper. (YES! That's right!)

Serves 6:

2 whole chickens
juice of 2 lemons
5 tbsp olive oil
salt (to taste)
2½ tbsp freshly ground black pepper

If one whole chicken, however small, seems extravagant for two people, wait until you taste it. (Besides, any leftovers are prime *planned obsolescence* material.) You could use two good segments if you wish to deprive yourself.

If you are using a whole chicken place it breast-down on a flat work surface and cut down the length of the back with a kitchen shears. Turn it over and cut through the wing and leg joints, where they join the body, without completely severing them. You want to get the carcase as flat as possible—a spatchcock chicken as it was once known. Give it a few friendly belts with the flat of a heavy cleaver if it won't lie down. Pull away any large pieces of fat before placing the chicken in a wide flat dish.

Mix the lemon juice, olive oil and black pepper (coarsely ground, not fine). Pour this mixture over and around the chicken as a marinade, making sure it covers the entire carcase. Turn the chicken in this regularly for 2 hours. In the fridge the chicken could be left to marinate all day or overnight.

The chicken can be cooked in several different ways. It can be grilled, but this requires a great deal of care to ensure even and complete cooking, roasted in a very hot oven or, best of all, barbecued over charcoal. All of these methods take 35-45 minutes depending upon the heat and the size of the chicken. The chicken should be crisp and brown on the outside but not burnt. Baste it frequently with the marinade. Oven temperature 220-230°C (425-450°F, gas mark 7-8). No matter which cooking method you choose always test to see that the juices are running clear from the thickest parts of the carcase, particularly the thigh. But it should still be juicy, not overcooked and dried out. Serve hot with a salad and homemade bread.

Puddings

Summer Pudding

Serves 2:

300 g soft fruit
1 tbsp sugar (optional)
4 thin slices of crustless stale white bread

Serves 6:

1 kilo soft fruit
3 tbsp sugar (optional)
12 slices bread

Choose a mixture of two or three fruits: raspberries, blackcurrants, strawberries, loganberries, black cherries, redcurrants, whortleberries. If you are using blackcurrants, redcurrants or whortleberries these fruits need to be simmered with the sugar for a minute to sweeten their slight tartness and to set their juices running. Once you have done this add the remaining fruits and briefly bring them to the heat. Set the pan aside.

Prepare the bread. It should be at least a day or two past freshness and old, soggy white pan will not work as it refuses to absorb the fruit juices and gives the pudding a texture like claggy soap. For individual servings, line ramekins, individual soufflé dishes or even a large teacup with the bread, slightly overlapping the edges and pressing them together at the joins. Spoon in the fruit mixture and either fold over the bread to make a lid or cut a separate lid from another slice of bread. You should reserve a little of the juice for later use. Cover the pudding with a slip of greaseproof paper and place a light weight on the puddings. (A tin of tuna fish works well.) Leave the puddings overnight in the fridge. Serve direct from the ramekins with whipped cream, or, more elegantly, turn out each pudding onto a pudding dish and pour over some of the reserved juice. Decorate with a fresh mint or borage leaf. Serve with whipped cream.

Fresh Figs with Walnuts and Goat's Cheese

One of my favourite ways of ending a meal.

Serves 2:

6 figs
6 shelled walnuts (optional)
2 slices of good goat's cheese

Good figs are dry with a sweet smell. You can eat the skin or it can be pulled off. Goat's cheese has a particular affinity with figs and so has *prosciutto* as a starter.

Crêpes with Fruit and Kirsch

Serves 2:

4-6 cooked crêpes
100 g strawberries
1 dsrtsp caster sugar
4 tbsp kirsch
100 g butter

Hull and slice the strawberries and sprinkle with the sugar. You could also use raspberries or loganberries. Divide the sugared fruit between the crêpes, place it on one-quarter of each crêpe before folding the crêpe over to form a triangular wedge. Use half the butter to grease a flat baking dish. Place the folded crêpes in the buttered baking dish. Melt the rest of the butter and pour it over the crêpes. Sprinkle with a little more of the sugar and place in the oven for 15 minutes at 190°C (375°F, gas mark 5). Just before serving, warm the kirsch, then pour it over the crêpes in the dish and set it alight with a match. Serve the crêpes at once, spooning the sauce over each serving.

Serves 6:

12-18 cooked crêpes
300 g strawberries
3 dsrtsp caster sugar
150 ml kirsch
250 g butter

Follow the instructions in the recipe for two people.

8

Cost-effective High Flying

Starters

Pasta Shells with Bacon and Tomato

Serves 2:

2 tbsp olive oil
100 g unsmoked bacon, salt pork, or Italian *pancetta*
130 g Italian tinned tomatoes
1 small onion (peeled and finely chopped)
1 fresh chilli (seeded and finely chopped)
40 g freshly grated grana-type cheese
200 g pasta shells or tubes

Serves 6:

4 tbsp olive oil
300 g unsmoked bacon, salt pork, or Italian *pancetta*
1 tin Italian tomatoes
2 medium onions (peeled and finely chopped)
2 fresh chillies (seeded and finely chopped)
100 g freshly grated grana-type cheese
500-600 g pasta shells or tubes

The bacon, salt pork, or *pancetta*, should be "in the piece" so that you can cut it into small cubes of about 1 cm. Cut the fat part of the bacon and the lean part into separate dice. If the bacon is very fat, and Italian *pancetta* often is, then you should use rather less olive oil than the recipe demands. Put oil into a pan with the cubes of fat and fry gently until the fat is brown and crisp. Remove the crisp fat with a slotted spoon and reserve. Add the lean diced bacon and the onion and cook them until the onion becomes translucent, now add the tomato and the chilli. Cook over a medium heat until any excess liquid has been driven off the tomatoes, the oil has separated out and you have a thick, red sauce. Just before serving add the crisped bacon fat to the sauce.

To cook the pasta, bring a large pot of water to a rolling boil, allowing a litre of water to each 100g of pasta. If the pasta is fresh, or fresh dried from a specialist shop, it will take about 2 to 3 minutes only to cook. Boil dried commercial brands for the length of time stated on the packet but begin testing them 2 minutes before the stated time is up. Pasta should never be overcooked until it is soft and sticky. It should be eaten *al dente* which means that it still has a bite to it. Pasta should be drained thoroughly the moment it is cooked and then placed at once in a warmed serving dish to which some warmed olive oil has been added. Give it a stir to coat the pasta with the oil. Now add the hot sauce and the grated cheese and mix them thoroughly. Serve and eat at once. Pasta cannot be kept waiting.

Hummus

Chick peas, puréed and flavoured with olive oil and tahina (a paste made from sesame seeds), is a favourite appetiser from the Middle East. Tahina is an acquired taste and I find that most recipes for *hummus bi tahina* recommend adding too much tahina for my taste. It is perfectly possible to make the dish without tahina or with the amount of tahina adjusted to your taste.

Serves 2:

150 g dried chick peas
1 clove garlic (peeled, crushed and finely chopped)
100 ml tahina paste (optional or use less (to taste))
1 tsp salt
juice of ½ lemon
1 tbsp good olive oil (or (to taste))
1 tbsp fresh chopped parsley
1 tsp ground paprika or ½ tsp ground roasted cumin
4-8 black olives
120 g feta cheese

Serves 6-8 :

450-500 g dried chick peas
3 cloves garlic (peeled, crushed and finely chopped)
200-300 ml tahina (optional or to taste)
3 tbsp olive oil (or slightly less to taste)
juice of 2 lemons
2-3 tsp salt
2 tbsp fresh chopped parsley
2 tsp ground paprika or 1½ tsp roasted ground cumin
12-24 black olives
350-400 g feta cheese

Soak the chick peas overnight in cold water. Drain and place the chick peas in a pot of cold water to cover. Bring to the boil, reduce heat and simmer for up to 2 hours until the peas are tender but not disintegrating. Replenish the water as needed. Skim off any scum which forms during cooking. When they are cooked, take up about a quarter-pint of the cooking water and retain it. Drain the chick peas. Put the peas, the olive oil, the salt and the garlic into the bowl of the food processor. Process until you have a smooth paste, adding just enough of the cooking water to achieve a soft (but not runny) consistency. Put the puréed peas into a bowl and mix in the tahina and the lemon juice. Add these in measured amounts until the taste is to your liking.

Use the paprika, or cumin, and the parsley to decorate the surface of the hummus. This is traditionally done by sprinkling the spices and the parsley in radial lines which segment the pale yellow surface of the purée.

Serve with hot home-baked pitta breads, the black olives, small cubes of the feta cheese and a green salad. The bread is torn apart and used to scoop up mouthfuls of the hummus. This is a substantial starter, and, by increasing the amount of salad, cheese, olives and bread, can become a perfectly reasonable, extremely healthy, main course.

Soups

I covered the basic principles of soup-making in my *Leaving Home Cookbook* and I have to admit that there are only three soups which I now make regularly at home: minestrone, wild mushroom, and nettle. I have nothing against soup but my family and most of my regular guests are not soup addicts and there is something about serving soup as a first course which suggests a lack of imagination, particularly when entertaining.

I give the recipe for minestrone here because I find it an invaluable stand-by and a hearty bowl works wonders on cold, winter days.

Minestrone Soup

This is a soup "more sinned against than sinning" and a good, genuine minestrone, served with home-made bread, can be a hearty meal on its own. It is not practical to make in small quantities (although this is perfectly possible) but stores well frozen, and, as long as you boil it up every day and store it in the fridge, improves in flavour for up to four days.

Serves 6:

3 small onions or leeks (peeled and finely chopped)
2 carrots
2 stalks celery
2 cloves garlic (peeled and crushed)
180 g dried cannellini or haricot beans
2 tbsp olive oil
1 tin Italian plum tomatoes
100 g *pancetta* or unsmoked streaky bacon (in the piece)
1 small green cabbage
1-1½ litres stock or water
salt and freshly ground black pepper (to taste)
2 tsp fresh chopped marjoram or ½ tsp dried oregano
1 tbsp fresh chopped parsley

Soak the beans in cold water overnight. Drain and cook in plenty of water until just tender. Do not drain. Depending on the beans they will take anywhere between 45 minutes and an hour. It is possible to buy good-quality canned, cooked, Italian cannellini beans and if you use these then you can omit this stage but will need to adjust the amount of stock.

Dice the *pancetta*, or bacon, and all the vegetables into a 1 cm dice. I prefer the soup made on young leeks rather than onions. Some recipes add turnip (or swede), spinach, potatoes, pasta, even green peas, but none of these is necessary. The beans are the thickening agent in this soup and so potatoes and pasta are redundant. Spinach can give a rather strong, even slightly sour, flavour to the soup but I sometimes add chopped spinach stems or swiss chard stems.

Sweat the diced vegetables and the diced bacon in the olive oil, slowly, over a low heat, for at least 20 minutes. Drain the tinned tomatoes into the stock and add the flesh of the tomatoes and the chopped marjoram to the sweated vegetables and stew this slowly for another 20 minutes. Season. Put half of the beans and some of their cooking water into the food processor and process until you get a thin purée. Add this purée, the whole beans and the remainder of their cooking liquid into the pot with the vegetables. Add the stock or water. Cover and simmer for an hour until all the vegetables are tender. Adjust the seasoning.

Fifteen minutes before serving add the cabbage and chopped parsley. Quarter the cabbage and remove the central stalk. Shred the rest as finely as possible.

Main Courses

Ladies' Thighs

This really is a splendid way to add Turkish delight to minced meat. The name comes from the shape into which you form the meat, which has become, as the Turks would say, smooth, soft and yielding! Well, Turkey is still a rather backward, male-dominated society.

Serves 2:

180 g minced lamb or beef
½ small onion (peeled and very finely chopped)
2 tbsp cooked long-grain rice

1 beaten egg
1 level tbsp grated feta cheese
1-2 tbsp plain flour
⅓ tsp ground (lightly roasted) cumin seeds
¼ tsp salt
¼ tsp freshly ground black pepper
pinch allspice

Serves 6:

560 g minced lamb or beef
1 large onion (peeled and very finely chopped)
6 tbsp cooked long-grain rice
1 large beaten egg
2 tbsp grated feta cheese
3 tbsp plain flour
1 tsp ground (lightly roasted) cumin seeds
½ sp salt
½ tsp freshly ground black pepper
good pinch allspice

These meatballs are called *koftas* in the Middle East and the meat is ground or minced twice so that it becomes almost a smooth paste. This effect can be achieved by processing good-quality minced meat in the food processor.

Put the meat, along with half the beaten egg, the salt, pepper, cumin and allspice, into the bowl of the processor. When it is almost a paste add the rice, onion and grated cheese, and process briefly, just enough to amalgamate all the extra ingredients into the paste.

Wet your hands in cold water, take a piece of the meat paste about the size of a golf ball and roll it into a ball and then press it gently between your palms to end up with something, admittedly rather vaguely, thigh-shaped. Do this until you have used up all the meat.

Heat 2-3 tablespoons of vegetable oil in a heavy-bottomed frying-pan. Dip the *koftas*, one at a time, into the flour and then into the beaten egg before frying them, five or six at a time, on both sides. Fry them until golden-brown and cooked through. Keep each batch warm, draining on kitchen paper, in the oven until you have them all cooked.

Serve them with garlic-and-lemon flavoured mayonnaise, plenty of freshly chopped thyme leaves, a green salad and hot, freshly baked pitta breads.

Beefburgers Stuffed with Mozzarella in a Pizzaiola Sauce

This dish has a rich, luscious texture and flavour which belies its humble ingredients. It is not really troublesome to prepare as both the meat and the sauce can be prepared ahead of time and stored in the fridge. It is good with plain boiled potatoes, Italian twice-cooked potatoes, or with freshly baked Italian flat bread to mop up the sauce.

Serves 2:

for the beefburgers:

240 g minced beef (neck or rib work well)
2 level tbsp fresh breadcrumbs
1 small beaten egg
50 g good-quality mozzarella cheese
1 tbsp olive oil

for the sauce:

1 small onion (peeled and very finely chopped)
1 clove garlic (peeled, crushed and finely chopped)
½ stalk of celery (very finely chopped)
1 tbsp celery leaves (finely chopped)
1 tsp tomato purée

200 g Italian tinned tomatoes
1 level tbsp fresh chopped marjoram or ½ tsp dried oregano
½ tsp sugar
salt and freshly ground black pepper (to taste)
1 tbsp olive oil

Serves 6:

for the beefburgers:

750 g minced beef
6 level tbsp fresh breadcrumbs
2 small beaten eggs
150 g good-quality mozzarella cheese
2 tbsp olive oil

for the sauce:

1 large onion (peeled and very finely chopped)
2 large cloves garlic (peeled, crushed and finely chopped)
1½ stalks celery (finely chopped)
2 tbsp celery leaves (finely chopped)
3 tsp tomato purée
600 g Italian tinned tomatoes
1½ tbsp fresh chopped marjoram or 1 tsp dried oregano
1½ tsp sugar
salt and freshly ground black pepper (to taste)
3 tbsp olive oil

To prepare the beefburgers, put the minced meat with the breadcrumbs and the beaten egg in a bowl. Season with a little freshly ground black pepper. Mix thoroughly. Divide the meat mixture into 4 (to serve two people) or 12 (for six) equal pieces and shape each into a flat burger shape about 1 cm thick. Cut the mozzarella cheese up into thin slices and divide it between half of the burgers, laying a layer on the top surface of the burger but leaving a clear space round the edge. Now place another burger shape on top of that containing the cheese. Wet your fingers and press lightly all round the edge to seal the cheese into the burgers. Put the stuffed burgers into the fridge until you are ready to cook them.

Prepare the sauce by heating the oil and then frying the onions, celery stalks and the garlic in it until the onions are soft and translucent. Add the tomatoes, tomato purée, marjoram, sugar, salt and plenty of freshly ground black pepper. Simmer for 15-25 minutes until the oil separates from the tomatoes and the sauce has reduced to a thick paste. You can store the sauce at this stage until you are ready to use it.

Fry the beefburgers in their olive oil until you have a good brown crust on both sides. (Don't burn them or overcook.) While you are doing this reheat the sauce. When the burgers are cooked, place them in a flat baking dish large enough to take them in a single layer. (Use two dishes if necessary.) Place the burgers in this and pour over the hot sauce. Deglaze the pan with a few tablespoons of water and pour the resulting juices into the sauce. Mix it in gently with a spoon. Cover tightly and cook in a medium oven for another 20 minutes.

Spanish Bean Stew

This delicious stew is a Spanish all-in-one boiled dinner or *cocido* and is the most popular everyday dish in the Spanish heartland. It varies, as all peasant dishes do, from region to region and from season to season using whatever local ingredients and vegetables are to hand. It appears under a variety of names too, the most common being *olla podrida*. The beans can be chick peas or, as in this recipe, a white bean like haricot or cannellini. It is not really worth making for two but makes a wonderful supper or informal dinner dish for six. It is served and eaten with lots of good home-made bread.

Serves 6:

500 g dried white beans
100 g good black pudding
100 g unsmoked streaky bacon (in the piece)
flesh of 1 red pepper
8-12 cloves garlic
3 tbsp olive oil
1 ham bone
100 g spicy sausage (chorizo)
250 g meat (chicken, pork, rabbit or beef)
500 g vegetables (mix onions, leeks, tomatoes, potatoes)
salt and freshly ground black pepper (to taste)
2 litres water

Soak the beans in cold water overnight. Cut the black pudding into six equal pieces. Remove the rind from the bacon piece and cut it up into 1 cm squares. Cut the bacon into bite-sized cubes. Remove the core and the seeds from the red pepper and cut the flesh into slices about 1 cm wide. The amount of garlic may seem excessive, but long-stewed garlic loses its characteristic flavour and becomes sweet and gentle. Do not panic, 12 cloves is roughly a whole head and in Spain they would not separate the cloves but simply char away the papery skin in a flame and add the whole head. This also releases the flavour.

Take a large stew-pot or casserole large enough to hold all the ingredients and heat the oil in it. Fry the bacon cubes gently in the oil for about 5 minutes. Drain the beans and discard the water. When the bacon is ready, add the ham bone, the beans, the whole head of garlic, the red pepper slices, Stir them to coat with the fat before adding 2 litres of water. Bring this to the boil and then turn down the heat and simmer the stew for about 2 hours. Depending on the beans it may take a little less than this or even a little longer to cook the beans. They should be tender but still firm. Now add the chorizos, cut into six serving pieces, and the meat. Cook for 20 minutes before adding the black pudding about half an hour before serving. The vegetables are added last, about 20 minutes before you intend to serve the stew. Just before you serve, stir in 1 tablespoon of olive oil and test the seasoning.

Serve in deep soup plates with lots of bread and a salad of sliced tomatoes and, in another dish, crisp lettuce leaves dressed with vinaigrette.

Herrings in Oatmeal

Now that herrings are readily available again, there can be absolutely no excuse for your not eating fish at least once a week. They are cheap, contain good quantities of the essential fatty acids which are so necessary for our bodily health, and, prepared as simply as in this recipe, quick to cook and serve. When the herring is in season this dish is a clear favourite fish in our household.

Serves 2:

4 small (or 2 large) herring fillets
2 tbsp butter
2 tbsp flour
4 tbsp oatflakes
1 beaten egg
2 lemon wedges
2 tbsp fresh chopped parsley

Serves 6:

12 small (or 6 large) herring fillets
6 tbsp butter
5 tbsp flour
12-14 tbsp oatflakes
3 beaten eggs
12 lemon wedges
4 tbsp fresh chopped parsley

This is one of those recipes which is utterly simple to prepare for two or three people but which can become complicated to prepare for larger numbers. However, it can be managed with a little help, two large pans and some juggling.

Wash and dry the herring fillets. Remove any obvious small bones, particularly the pin bones about half-way between the edges of the fillet and where the backbone was. I am told that I am overly cautious in this regard. My husband, who would quite happily eat these herring seven days a week, just chews them bones and all.

Dip the herring fillets in the flour on both sides, then in the beaten egg, and then in the oatflakes. Make sure that the oatflakes completely cover the herring fillets on both sides, pressing them onto the surface with your fingers if necessary. The fish can be stored in the fridge for several hours at this point.

Heat the butter in a heavy-bottomed frying-pan and just as it foams add the herring fillets. Cook over a medium heat until the oatflakes are evenly browned but not burnt. This will take 3-5 minutes depending upon the heat and the thickness of the fish. Turn the fillets over and cook on the second side for the same time. It is possible, if you are cooking them in batches, to keep the fish warm, draining on kitchen paper, in a low oven. Serve with lemon wedges, a good sprinkling of fresh chopped parsley, and good home-made brown bread and butter. Boiled potatoes would be a more traditional accompaniment.

Puddings

We are not great eaters of hot puddings. All three of us prefer cold fruit puddings or just fresh fruit. When I am asked for a hot pudding it will always be one of these two recipes. Middle-aged businessmen seem to find them hard to resist as well—nostalgic puddings perhaps?

Bread and Butter Pudding
Banish all memories of the grey, wet, stodgy mushes so beloved of school cooks. This pudding is delicious and, now that you are making your own bread regularly, is a perfect way of using up those bits and bobs that escape.

Serves 2:

6 slices of day-old (at least) bread
butter (to taste)
1 tbsp raisins
1 large egg
150 ml full cream milk
2 tsp grated lemon rind
2 tsp grated orange rind

Serves 6:

18 slices bread
butter (to taste)
3 tbsp raisins
3 eggs
450 ml full cream milk
grated rind of 1 lemon
grated rind of 1 orange

Cut the crusts from the bread and butter each slice. Cut the slices into triangular shapes. (Not absolutely necessary.) Butter a baking dish just large enough to hold all the slices in overlapping layers and scatter the raisins between the layers as you arrange the bread. Separate the egg yolks from the whites. Warm the milk and then whisk the yolks into the milk. Whisk the egg whites until they are stiff and then fold them carefully into the milk and egg mixture. Pour this over the bread and scatter half of the grated citrus rind over the surface. Bake in a preheated oven at 190°C (375°F, gas mark 5) for 30 minutes for a small pudding and 40-45 minutes for a larger one. The pudding should be set and golden-brown. Sprinkle with the rest of the rind just before serving.

Treacle Tart

This is definitely for people with a sweet tooth. Slices of it freeze quite well if they are well and carefully wrapped. They can be thawed in the microwave and reheated in the oven. Do not reheat them in the microwave, however, as the treacle tends to burn easily.

for the shortcrust pastry:

200 g plain pastry flour
pinch of salt
100 g butter or margarine
2-3 tbsp ice-cold water

for the filling:

4 tbsp golden syrup
2 tbsp butter
2 tbsp cream
1 small cooking apple (peeled, cored and grated)

Cut the butter or margarine into 1 cm cubes and sift the flour directly into the bowl of the food processor. Add the fat and process until it is well blended into the flour. Dribble 2 tbsp of water and process again. If it does not cling together after 20 seconds sprinkle in a little more water until it does. Turn out onto a flat floured surface and knead just enough to form into a ball. Rest in the fridge for at least 15 minutes.

Roll out the pastry and line a flat baking tin with it. Decorate the edges or not as you will. In a bowl in the microwave, or a small pot on the stove, warm the syrup until it runs. Do not overheat. Add the cream, apple and all but a dessertspoonful of the butter. Mix well. Brush the remaining butter over the bottom of the flan and pour in the mixture to cover the pastry.

Bake in a preheated oven at 180°C (365°F, gas mark 4-5) for 30 minutes. Allow the tart to cool for 2 or 3 minutes before serving with whipped cream.

9

Who's Coming to Dinner?

There will be occasions when you would like to entertain formally in your home. Eating out is expensive and the food for which you pay exorbitant prices rarely reaches a standard which justifies the cost. Whether you are called upon to entertain for reasons of business or from economic necessity, an inexperienced cook can feel intimidated by the whole prospect of planning and preparing a formal luncheon or dinner party. This section of the book allows you to entertain guests in your home with food which is out of the ordinary but well within the abilities of anyone who has worked through the earlier chapters.

I have, in the main, chosen dishes which can be prepared ahead of time, and which require your presence in the kitchen as little as possible immediately before or during the meal. Almost all the starters and puddings are cold and the main courses are all dishes which will not come to any harm if they are kept waiting for a while. The vegetable dishes are all prepared ahead of time and will not spoil easily. Ingredients are for six. This is not an arbitrary number but settled on as being small enough not to intimidate the cook, but large enough to allow for you to have two of your own friends along when your partner invites the boss and her husband.

Most of the recipes in earlier sections can be served

when you are entertaining at home. (With the obvious exception of those which I have specifically said are difficult to manage for more than two people.) Don't forget to serve a suitable home-made bread.

Nibbles

No need to go mad here, but it is a good idea to hand round something to nibble with the drinks when guests first arrive. If they are home-made and delicious then your dinner party is off to a good start before it has properly begun.

Salted Almonds

I warn you not to make too many salted almonds. My guests always eat every last one of them no matter how many I make. They are supposed to lessen the effects of strong drink but I take that with a grain of the salt they are dusted with.

Serves 6:

350 g whole blanched almonds
2 tbsp sea salt
2 tbsp sunflower oil
2 tsp almond oil (optional)

Oil a large baking tray with the oils and spread the whole blanched almonds out in a single layer. Place the tray into the oven at 150°C (300°F, gas mark 2) for about 15 minutes. Almonds scorch easily so keep a close eye on them, shaking them from time to time. When they are an even light golden-brown remove them from the oven and let them cool for a minute or two. Crush the sea salt finely and place it in a paper bag. Put the almonds into the paper bag and shake them until they are dusted with the salt. Serve cold, in a suitable dish.

Quail Eggs with Celery Salt

Serves 6:

12 quail eggs
1 tsp celery seed
3 tsp sea salt

I serve these as a rather substantial nibble with drinks. The eggs are very small, and although the pretty little shells are half their attraction, it is better to shell them before you serve them. Boil the eggs in water for 5 minutes. Cool them at once by plunging them into cold running water.

Make the celery salt by crushing together the celery seeds with the sea salt with a mortar and pestle. This is used as a dry dip for the eggs, so pass them round together.

Constructing Menus

It is important not to let ambition overreach itself when you are constructing menus for luncheon or dinner parties. Recipes which are a doddle for two and quite manageable for four people can become mind-bogglingly difficult when you attempt to cook them for six!

You must always allow for the fact that you will need to greet and talk to your guests, serve and refresh their drinks, as well as dish up a meal to them. Furthermore, someone will always be late, drunk, a vegetarian, kosher, diabetic or allergic to an ingredient in the main course. If you are entertaining people you do not know well, then it makes sense (however much it may seem like a counsel of perfection) to have a stand-by dish ready in the fridge which can be quickly microwaved into readiness. I find vegetarians the most common spanner in the works, so I always have a vegetarian dish under starter's orders. Many people dislike shellfish, so if you are serving them have an alternative to hand. If you are serving pork, it makes sense to have an alternative as well. Perhaps it is better to avoid pork and shellfish altogether if you do not know your guests well. Have fruit and cheese for non-pudding eaters and those on strict diets and always have sufficient good, non-alcoholic beverages for drivers and non-drinkers.

As for what you serve your guests, use your common sense. Try to avoid repetitive flavours or ingredients—do not serve a succession of dishes which have cream as a basic ingredient, or a tomato-based soup followed by a main course with a tomato-based sauce. Vary the texture of the food you serve, both within the individual courses and through the successive courses—no menus with thick, creamy soup, followed by soft, puréed vegetables to accompany a casserole, followed by a mushy pudding.

If I try to follow one rule above all others it is, as far as possible, to allow things to taste like themselves. And this principle should be carried through into menu-planning. I think this is why I prefer Italian and Greek food to French food, and what might be termed *peasant* dishes to those from the *haute cuisine* or *cordon bleu* traditions. There are no cast-iron rules in menu-planning, but it makes sense not to serve fiery-spiced dishes before a delicate fish dish, or to allow the main meat or fish to be overpowered by the accompaniments.

Many of the ideas about menu-planning were formulated in the days when meals were made up of many successive courses. Today, I rarely serve more than three courses, and hardly ever serve both a soup and a fish course as well as a meat course. It is quite permissible to serve, as the Italians do, two courses of equal size, rather than a main course flanked by two smaller ones. I often serve an Indian or Chinese vegetable dish as an accompaniment to a European meat recipe, but these combinations are the result of much experimentation and would not necessarily be to the taste of others.

The four menus which follow are no more than suggestions and there are other ways of mixing and matching the recipes.

Menu I

Sole with Crisp Vegetables and a Sweet and Sour Sauce
Roast Venison with Game Sauce
Braised Red Cabbage
Purée of Chestnuts and Potato
Syllabub with Biscuit

Menu II

Scallops with Wine, Herbs and Garlic
Rack of Lamb (Crown Roast)
Potatoes with Cream
Purée of Leeks
Dried Fruit Salad

Menu III

Stuffed Vine Leaves
Osso Bucco
Polenta
Fruit Fool

Menu IV

Indian Grilled Chicken Strips
Vegetable Biryani
Boiled Rice

Tomato and Onion Relish
Cucumber Raita
Chapattis and Naans

Menu I

Sole with Crisp Vegetables and a Sweet and Sour Sauce

This dish is eaten cold and is fully cooked two days in advance, stored in the fridge and brought up to room temperature before serving. It has a spicy, Middle Eastern flavour.

Serves 2:

Use one-third of the fish and half the rest of the ingredients.

Serves 6:

6 fillets of slip sole
30 g flour
120 ml olive oil

for the dressing and garnish:

1 carrot
1 onion
1 stick celery
50 ml white wine
50 ml wine vinegar
50 g sultanas
½ tsp ground cinnamon
3 whole cloves
3 bay leaves
salt and freshly ground black pepper (to taste)

Cut each fillet of sole in half lengthways. Season the flour with a little salt and pepper and coat each piece of fish with it, making sure to shake off any excess flour. Heat 100 ml of the oil in a pan and fry the fishes, on both sides, until the flesh is opaque and flakes easily. This will take about 2-3 minutes per side depending on the size and thickness of the fishes. Drain the fishes on kitchen paper before laying in a wide shallow dish which will take the fishes in a single layer.

Slice the vegetables very thinly and stir-fry them in the remaining oil in a clean pan. When they are just beginning to colour and soften, season them, add the wine and the vinegar and cook briskly until this liquid has reduced by half. Add the sultanas, cloves, cinnamon and bay leaves and then pour this sauce over the fish, covering it as evenly as possible. Cover and leave to marinate for 48 hours.

Roast Venison

Today, farmed venison is beginning to make an impact on the market because it is a lean meat, and in some minds, therefore, "healthier," and significantly less expensive than beef or lamb. We eat quite a lot of wild venison because we have a sporting friend. It can be uncertain of age and may need tenderising and slow cooking. Farmed venison is always killed young and is always tender. Deer meat is so lean that it must always be "larded" to prevent it drying out during roasting or grilling. It is quite usual to marinate even farmed venison for a day or two.

Serves 6:

2-3 lb haunch of venison
6 oz bacon or pork fat
sheets of flead fat to cover or 4 oz pork dripping

for the marinade:

1 cup wine or cider vinegar
2 cups dry white wine
½ cup olive oil
1 large onion (sliced)
2 carrots (sliced)
3 large sprigs parsley
3 sprigs fresh thyme
6 crushed black peppercorns
6 crushed juniper berries
1 tsp salt

Make sure that your game dealer removes the outer membrane and draws the sinews from the haunch. Cut the bacon or pork fat into thin strips and use a larding needle to insert it into the haunch. When you are finished the haunch should have the look of a bald, blunt hedgehog. Mix all the ingredients for the marinade in a large bowl and immerse the haunch completely. It needs at least 8-12 hours to marinate and if you are at all doubtful of the beast's age then give it 24-36 hours in a cool place. Turn the joint frequently in the marinade.

When you are ready to cook it remove it from the marinade and dry it completely with kitchen paper. If you can get sheets of flead pork fat then tie these round the joint so that at least the top of the joint is completely wrapped in fat. If you are using dripping then render it down and paint the joint with about half of the fat. Roast in a preheated oven on a rack at 180°C (350°F, gas mark 4) for 20 minutes to the pound plus 20 minutes over. With regular basting, this should produce a joint which is still on the rare side which is the way venison is served in Ireland. If you prefer it well done then roast it for 30 minutes to the pound plus 20 minutes more. If you have a joint which weighs more than 4 lb then reduce the cooking-time to 15 minutes per pound (rare) and no more than 25 minutes per pound (well done).

Game Sauce

This is a very useful sauce to accompany a number of game dishes.

Serves 6:

1 tbsp finely chopped carrot
1 tbsp finely chopped onion
1 tbsp finely chopped celery
2 tbsp good olive oil
1 tbsp flour
2 cups good meat bone stock
1-2 tbsp rowan or redcurrant jelly

Heat the oil and gently sweat the vegetables in it until they are soft and just beginning to brown at the edges. Add the flour and cook it until it is brown but not burnt. Add the stock to the pan and allow it to simmer for 40 minutes. Keep it well stirred. Skim it, strain it and return the thickened sauce to the pan with the rowan or redcurrant jelly. Stir it over a gentle heat until the jelly has completely integrated.

To serve this sauce with the venison you should thinly slice the meat having first removed the outer fat wrapping. Pour a small amount of the sauce over the sliced meat and serve the rest of the sauce at table. Accompany the meat with what our guests always refer to as "posh fried bread"—croutons of thinly sliced bread fried until golden and crisp in a mixture of butter and good, fruity olive oil. These can be prepared in advance and kept warm in the bottom of the oven between layers of absorbent kitchen paper. I always serve a little dish of the jelly used to flavour the sauce.

Rowan Jelly

In Ireland the rowan tree is called the mountain ash. The Celts made wine from its bright scarlet berries and used them to flavour mead. It is a traditional accompaniment to venison and game birds. It used to be necessary to go up into the hills to collect the ripe berries but now you can see them in most suburban streets and gardens. I think I'd still be inclined to gather mine in the countryside as far away from traffic fumes as possible.

3 lb ripe red rowan berries
2 lb cooking apples (crab if possible)
4-5 cups water
1-2 lb sugar

Place the berries, the apples (washed but not peeled) into a pot with about 5 cups of water. Bring this to the boil and boil it for another 40 minutes. Strain the contents of the pot overnight through a jelly bag. Measure the juice which passes through into the bowl. You will need 1 lb of sugar for each 2½ cups of juice. Boil the juice in a heavy-bottomed pot for 10 minutes then add the correct amount of warmed sugar. Boil again for about 10 more minutes, skimming off any scum which forms. Test for setting in the usual way and when the setting is right pour the jelly into sterilised jars and seal them at once. This stores almost indefinitely as long as the seal remains intact.

I also make a jelly from ripe elderberries using this method and flavour it with fresh, lightly bruised, thyme leaves.

1 red cabbage
2 large onions (peeled and chopped)
4 tbsp vegetable oil
150 g *pancetta* or unsmoked streaky bacon (in the piece)
30 ml wine vinegar
2 tbsp tomato purée
50 ml water
salt and freshly ground black pepper (to taste)

Cut the cabbage into four, removing any damaged outer leaves. Cut out the tough core and slice the rest of the leaves into strips about 1 cm wide. Now chop these strips in two or three. Mix the tomato purée with the water. Fry the chopped onion and the finely chopped *pancetta* in the oil in a wide pan until the onion is soft and translucent. Add the vinegar to the pan and allow it to bubble for a minute. Add the red cabbage to the pan and stir-fry it for 2 minutes. Now add the diluted tomato purée to the pan and season. Bring the liquid to the boil then transfer the contents of the pan to a suitable casserole with a tight-fitting lid. Cook this on the floor of the oven for 2 hours. (It is possible to cook it on top of the stove but you must check it regularly to see that some liquid remains.)

Purée of Chestnuts and Potato

Fresh whole chestnuts are very troublesome and I have long since given up buying them. I buy tins of whole chestnuts in brine. The sweetened, tinned dessert chestnuts are not suitable.

Serves 6:

2 tins whole chestnuts
750 g potato

60 g butter
salt and freshly ground black pepper (to taste)

Boil the potatoes in their jackets and then peel them. While still hot, add the butter and season them before working them through a mouli-sieve. Drain the brine from the chestnuts and wash them briefly under running water. Work the chestnuts through the mouli. (The food processor is not really suitable for this.) Now mix the potato and chestnut together and pass the mixture through the mouli once more. Spoon the mixture into six ramekins. These can be baked below the venison for 10-15 minutes. If it is more convenient they can be heated through in the microwave until hot just before serving them.

Syllabub with Biscuit

This luscious pudding is prepared the day before it is served, and while it is very rich, only small amounts are served in a small glass. This dish (its name means "frothy") was made originally by milking the cow directly into a dish containing brandy—the result was a frothy pudding.

Serves 6:

200 ml cream
juice and grated rind of 1 medium lemon
1 tbsp brandy
4 tbsp dry sherry
1 tbsp caster sugar.

Grate the rind from the lemon into a bowl before extracting its juice and putting this into the bowl mixed with the brandy, sherry and sugar. Stir this mixture until the sugar has completely dissolved. Beat the cream with a whisk or hand-held electric beater until it is just beginning to thicken. Slowly, add the lemon and sherry mixture, whisking all the time. Keep whisking until the mixture is light and fluffy. Spoon into glasses and chill overnight in the fridge. I like to decorate this pudding with a single blue borage flower.

It can be served on its own or with a crisp sweet biscuit.

Biscuits

2 beaten eggs
250 g self-raising flour
150 g caster sugar
30 ml sunflower oil
pinch of salt
grated rind of half a lemon

Stir the eggs and oil together with the grated lemon rind, add the sugar and then the sieved flour and salt. Mix to a soft dough. Oil a baking sheet and onto this drop teaspoonsful of the dough, making sure that each piece of dough is 4 cm away from its nearest neighbour. (They spread in cooking.) Flatten each piece lightly with oiled fingers or the base of a jar which has been oiled. Bake at 175°C (350°F, gas mark 4) for 8-10 minutes. Like all biscuits, these harden as they cool, so do not overcook them.

Menu II

Scallops with Wine, Herbs and Garlic

This dish can be prepared a day in advance and gratinéed just before serving. The number of scallops you will need depends very much on their size. I prefer the small queen scallops and would usually allow four of these per person.

The commonest size are medium and two of these should be sufficient. Very large scallops can contain a great deal of flesh and one of these per person would be enough.

Serves 6:

6, 12, or 24 scallops depending upon size
1 large onion (peeled, finely chopped)
1 clove garlic (peeled, crushed and finely chopped)
90 g butter
100 g flour
1 tbsp olive oil
2 tbsp grated Swiss Gruyère cheese
150 ml white wine
1 bay leaf
good pinch of fresh, chopped thyme

Prepare the scallops by opening the shells with an oyster knife and removing the flesh into a bowl of water. Extract the white flesh and the orange-coloured coral, and discard the dark organs and the fringe-like membrane. There is a small, crescent-shaped muscle with a dark line through it which should be cut away as it is tough and leathery. Leave small queen scallops intact but cut up the flesh of medium and large scallops into slices ½ cm thick. With a scallop in front of you these instructions will make sense, believe me.

Dry the flesh on kitchen paper and just before cooking dredge lightly in the flour, shaking off the excess. Fry the onion and garlic in 30 g of the butter and olive oil until the onions are translucent. Remove the onions and garlic with a slotted spoon and reserve. Fry the floured scallops in another 30 g of the butter for about 2 minutes until they are lightly browned and then pour the wine into the pan. Add the cooked onion and garlic and the herbs and simmer, covered, for no more than 5 minutes. Uncover and boil the sauce until it has thickened slightly, season to taste, and discard the bay leaf. Spoon the scallops with the sauce into six serving bowls or into six, cleaned large scallop shells. Sprinkle with the grated cheese and dot with the remaining 30 g of butter. Place the dishes in the fridge. Six minutes before serving, reheat in the microwave for 2 minutes on the medium setting before browning the top under a hot grill for another 2 minutes. You can skip the microwave and reheat them for 4 minutes under the grill but do ensure that they are heated through.

Crown Roast of Lamb

You will usually need to order the meat from your butchers a few days in advance. Ask him to cut two fair ends, remove the papery outside skin and to chine the joints (remove the backbone) and tie the joint into a crown.

Serves 6 (8 at a pinch):

- 2 fair ends of lamb (1½-2 kilo in total) in a crown roast
- 1 tbsp water
- 1 dsrtsp Dijon mustard
- 2 tsp salt
- 1 tsp freshly ground black pepper

Make a paste with the mustard, water, salt and pepper and paint the lamb with it, using a pastry brush. Place the lamb into a preheated oven at 200°C (400°F, gas mark 6) for one and a quarter hours. This will give you lamb which is still pink and juicy (which is how you should eat it).

Traditionally the centre of this roast was stuffed with vegetables or a farced stuffing. I'm against this because it can mean either that the lamb gets overcooked in order thoroughly to cook the farce stuffing, or, if it is a vegetable garnish (carrots and peas or mushrooms in a cream sauce, or spinach braised with butter were usual), the garnish and its sauce get in the way of carving. By all means put the vegetables into the centre of the roast if that appeals to you, but cook them separately first.

Potatoes with Cream

This is a classic French accompaniment to roast lamb and it goes well with almost any grilled or roasted meat or poultry.

Serves 6:

1 kilo potatoes (peeled and cut into ¼ cm slices)
60 g butter
300 ml fresh cream
1 clove garlic (peeled, crushed and finely chopped)
3 tbsp Gruyère cheese (or a mixture of Gruyère and a grana type)
salt and freshly ground black pepper (to taste)

Use 30 g of the butter to grease a flat baking dish. Layer the potato slices with a little of the garlic, seasoning and cheese. (The cheese in this dish is optional. It is perfectly good without it.) Pour over the cream and dot the top with small cubes of the remaining butter. Bring the dish to a slow simmer on top of the stove before placing it on the lowest shelf of the oven with the lamb (200°C, 400°F, gas mark 6). Cook for 1-1¼ hours. The cream will be just absorbed by the potatoes and the top layer brown and crisp. If it is browning too quickly then cover it with a layer of foil for part of the cooking-time. You can peel and slice the potatoes ahead of time and store them under cold water in a bowl.

Purée of Leeks

This dish can be prepared a day early and reheated. It is an ideal dinner-party dish because it does not mind hanging around.

Serves 6:

1.5 kilos leeks
60 g butter
a pinch of grated nutmeg
salt and freshly ground black pepper (to taste)

Trim off the excess green leaves from the leeks down to where they form a tight roll. (Keep these for adding to soup.) Thoroughly clean the leeks making sure to dislodge any earth which has lodged in the space where the green leaves join the white part and removing any damaged outer skins from the white part of the vegetables. Chop the leeks into 3 cm chunks and cover them in a pot with cold water. Bring the water to the boil and simmer the leeks for 15 minutes. Drain off the water and put the leeks into the bowl of the food processor with the butter and seasonings. Process to a purée and pack this into individual ramekins. Reheat the leeks in the oven with the lamb for about 15-20 minutes or in the microwave for 3-5 minutes.

Dried Fruit Salad

500-700 g mixed dried fruits (apricots, prunes, figs, apples and peaches)
2 tbsp barbados brown sugar (optional)
2 tbsp raisins
30 g chopped almonds
60 g chopped walnuts
grated rind and juice of 2 oranges
grated rind and juice of 1 lemon

This pudding can be prepared ahead of time. Cover all the dried fruit except the raisins with water and soak for 1 hour. Put the fruits, and enough of the water in which they were soaking to cover, into a pot. Bring this to heat and simmer for 12-15 minutes until they are soft but not disintegrating. Remove the pot from the heat and add the brown sugar if you are using it. I leave it out because it makes the pudding far too sweet for my taste. Add the raisins and the grated citrus rinds. Allow to cool completely and then add the citrus juices and the chopped nuts.

Menu III

Cold Stuffed Vine Leaves (Dolmáthes)

Vine leaves can be bought preserved in brine. They are very fragrant and make a delicious cold starter. It is possible to use cabbage leaves for this recipe but they are never anything but a substitute. If you do use cabbage leaves choose young tender leaves and remove the tough central stem, then blanch and soften them in boiling salted water for about a minute before folding them round the stuffing.

Serves 6 (24 *dolmáthes*):

110 ml olive oil
2 onions (peeled and very finely chopped)
3 spring onions (very finely chopped)
½ tsp salt
¼ tsp ground black pepper
1 tbsp pine kernels
1 tbsp finely chopped fresh dill leaves
4 tbsp finely chopped fresh parsley
1 tsp finely chopped fresh mint leaves

3 tbsp lemon juice
24 vine leaves (or blanched young cabbage leaves)
⅔ cup long-grain rice
16-18 floz water
enough parsley sprigs to cover the bottom of a pot

Heat half of the olive oil and sauté the onions and spring onions until soft and transparent. Add salt, pepper, pine nuts and the rice. Cook for 10 minutes stirring occasionally. Add the dill, mint, 2 tablespoons of lemon juice and 6 fluid ounces of water. Cover and simmer until the liquid is absorbed (about 10 minutes). The rice will be slightly undercooked.

Drain the vine leaves and rinse them in several changes of cold water. Drain. Blanch the vine leaves in boiling water for 1 minute. When they are cool enough to handle, separate them and spread them out gently on a flat surface. Cut out any thick stems.

Place a heaped teaspoon of the filling at the base of the dull underside of a leaf. Fold up the bottom, then fold in the sides; now roll up towards the point of the leaf. This should give you a small sausage shape. Repeat until you have used up all the stuffing or exhausted your supply of leaves. Do not wrap too tightly, because the rice must expand as it cooks.

Place the stuffed leaves, packed closely, with the open edge of the fold held shut by its neighbour, on top of the parsley sprigs in the cooking pot. When you have covered the whole bottom surface of the pot place the stuffed leaves in a second layer on top of the first.

Mix the remaining oil, 2 tablespoons of lemon juice and 10-12 fluid ounces of water, and add this mixture carefully to the pot containing the *dolmáthes*. Place a plate, inverted, over the *dolmáthes* to prevent them moving while cooking. The water should barely cover the plate. Cover the pot and bring to the boil. Reduce the heat and simmer for 1½ hours until most of the liquid is absorbed. Remove the pot from the heat and allow the *dolmáthes* to cool completely for at least 2 hours, or even overnight.

Remove the plate from the pot, and set the *dolmáthes* on a serving plate, carefully, one at a time, so that they do not tear or unravel. Serve slightly chilled with a squeeze of lemon juice over them.

Osso Bucco

One of those marvellously rich Italian stews which can be left cooking gently for hours. You may have to order the veal shin in advance from your butcher. Ask him for a hind shin and get him to saw it into 5 cm thick cuts across the bone, and remove the outer skin. This is a marrowbone and is left in the centre of each piece. Each piece should be bound with string or tape round the middle to keep it in shape during cooking.

Serves 6:

for the stew:

12 pieces of 5 cm thick veal shin (about 3 whole shins)
3 onions (peeled and finely chopped)
2 carrots (very finely diced)
2 sticks celery (finely diced)
50 g butter
1 large clove garlic (peeled, crushed and finely chopped)
100 g plain flour
250 ml dry white wine
300 ml veal or chicken stock
2 sprigs parsley

2 bay leaves
salt and freshly ground black pepper (to taste)

for the *gremolada* garnish:

2 level tsp finely grated lemon rind
1 small clove garlic (peeled, crushed and finely chopped)
2 tbsp very finely chopped fresh parsley

Sweat the onion, carrot and celery in 30 g of the butter for 10-15 minutes, over a low heat. Lift these vegetables out of the pan with a slotted spoon and put them in a layer over the bottom of a casserole large enough to take all of the meat in one layer.

Dust the veal pieces in the flour and shake off any excess. Add the remaining butter to the pan in which the vegetables were cooked and, over a medium heat, seal and brown the veal pieces on all sides. Put the browned meat pieces in a single layer into the casserole on top of the vegetables. Deglaze the frying-pan with the wine, allowing it to bubble and reduce slightly while you scrape off the residue on the pan into the sauce. Add the wine sauce to the casserole. Bring the meat stock to the boil in the frying-pan and add this to the casserole. Add the bay leaves and the sprigs of parsley.

Place the casserole into a preheated oven at 150°C (300°F, gas mark 2) and cook for 2 hours. The lid of the casserole must be a good fit to prevent evaporation of the sauce. If it is not, seal it with a layer of kitchen foil and be prepared to top up the stewing liquid with stock if it needs it.

Just before serving, mix the grated lemon rind, finely chopped garlic and parsley together to make the garnish. Remove the individual pieces of veal from the casserole, one by one, into a very hot serving dish, and remove the string. Pour the sauce round the veal pieces and garnish each piece of meat with a little of the *gremolada*.

Traditionally, *osso bucco* is served with a risotto. I find the preparation of risotto far too complicated when you have guests to attend to, and reheated risotto is not my idea of heaven. I usually serve it with lashings of hot focaccia bread and encourage my guests to abandon all decorum and dunk the torn bread into the glorious gravy. The marrowbone at the centre of each piece of veal should be sucked clean and you should have finger bowls of hot water and plenty of paper napkins for each guest.

If you feel that you do not know your guests well enough to ask them to do this then either serve something else, or serve some grilled or baked *polenta* as an accompaniment.

Polenta

Polenta is the classic food of the poor in that part of northern Italy around the delta of the River Po. Today, it is a mixture of coarsely ground maize flour and water; but in antiquity it was made from *spelt*, a kind of wheat, and other cereals. The name comes from the Latin *puls* or *pulmentum*. Prepare the *polenta* the day before you intend to serve it and when it is cold cut it into slices 15 cm long, 2 cm wide and 1½ -2 cm thick. These can then be painted with olive oil and grilled, baked, or fried until a crisp crust forms. Serve a slice with each serving of the *osso bucco*.

Serves 6:

300 g ground maize
1 level tbsp salt
1.75 litres boiling water

Bring the water to a boil in a large saucepan, add the

salt and turn down the heat. The water should be only simmering when you add the ground maize. Add it in a thin stream from your fist, stirring constantly as you do so. After all the flour has been added, continue stirring for 10 minutes. After that you can get on with other jobs as long as you give the *polenta* a good strong stir every minute or so. Cook it for at least 40 minutes.

Turn the *polenta* onto a wooden board onto which you have laid out a clean table napkin or tea-towel. The polenta is ready to eat or to be allowed to cool before being cooked again.

This will make more than you need for your dinner party, but it keeps well for a few days in the fridge and can be fried in the pan as an accompaniment for bacon and eggs or used as a snack, by cutting it into flat slices which are then dressed with a pizza topping and baked in the oven. It has a very strong flavour which stands up well to the equally rich *osso bucco*.

Fruit Fool

Personally, I would not serve a pudding with this meal. Some good fresh fruit or even a cleansing salad would be quite sufficient. But I do realise that many people feel they have been denied if they do not get a pudding. This is simple and can be prepared in advance.

Serves 6 :

750 g of fruit in season (gooseberries, apples, apricots)
2-3 tbsp sugar (depending on taste or the tartness of the fruit)
300 ml fresh whipped cream

Stew the fruit in 3 tablespoons of water until soft. Add

the sugar and taste. Purée in the food processor or mouli-sieve before folding into the lightly whipped cream. Spoon into small serving glasses or dishes. Serve lightly chilled.

Menu IV

An Indian Dinner

While I am firmly wedded to what might be loosely called Mediterranean peasant food, my husband, who is no mean cook, says that if he had to live with only one cuisine he would choose Indian. He has been madly in love with Madhur Jaffrey ever since he bought her classic *Invitation to Indian Cooking* about fifteen years ago, long before her first television series (which merely served to confirm him in his loyalty).

None of the dishes I have chosen for this dinner-party meal is difficult to prepare (once you have assembled the ingredients and spices) and none of them is *hot*. Spicy, yes, but fiery, no. The meal is not divided up into courses as all the dishes are intended to be served together. The recipes for the two breads, *chapattis* and *naans* appeared in the chapter about bread. That for the chicken strips is from Madhur Jaffrey's marvellous book (which should be on every cook's shelf) and the vegetable biryani is dish which has developed in our kitchen over years of experimentation. As a meal it is not really practicable to prepare for just two people but I suggest that you try it out on close friends before you rush into preparing it for guests whom you wish to impress.

Indian Grilled Chicken Strips

Serves 6:

6 chicken supremes (boned, skinned, single breasts)
5 tbsp olive oil
4 tbsp red wine vinegar
1 onion (peeled and chopped)
8-12 cloves garlic (peeled, crushed and chopped)
2 cm cube of fresh root ginger (peeled and chopped)
2 tbsp whole fennel seeds
2 tbsp ground cumin seeds
8 cardamom pods (seeds from)
2 tsp ground coriander seeds
1 tsp ground cinnamon
8 whole cloves
20 black peppercorns
½ tsp (level) cayenne pepper
2 tsp salt
1 tbsp tomato purée

Prepare the onions, garlic and root ginger. Remove the skins from the chicken breasts, dry them and cut the breasts up lengthways into thin strips about 1 cm wide.

Take all the whole spices and grind them together in a mortar or, best of all, in the head of a small electric coffee grinder kept solely for spices. Be sure to remove the outer pod from the cardamoms and use only the tiny black seeds. I always add the cayenne and the salt when I am grinding the other ingredients.

Put the chopped onion, garlic and ginger, together with the oil, the vinegar and the tomato purée, into the bowl of the food processor and blend until you have a thick smooth paste. Add all the spices and give it a quick process to mix them through the paste. Place the chicken strips into a bowl containing the paste. Mix well and use your fingers to massage the marinade gently into the chicken pieces. Put the bowl into the fridge and let the chicken marinate for at least 5 hours. I have left them overnight without them coming to any harm.

Three-quarters of an hour before you intend to serve the meal cook the chicken strips under a preheated grill. Cover the tray of the grill-pan with cooking foil to catch the drips. Cook the chicken for about 10 minutes on one side before turning it over to cook for an equal length of time on the second. You should not crowd the chicken pieces together and will probably need to cook them in two batches. Keep the first batch warm while you cook the second. They should not be evenly browned but only be dark in patches. Serve the chicken on a dish lined with crisp lettuce leaves.

This chicken is equally delicious cold or as a picnic snack.

Vegetable Biryani

Serves 6:

600 g French beans
1 small head cauliflower (divided into florets)
1 aubergine or 4-6 small courgettes
2 onions (peeled and roughly chopped)
2 onions (peeled, cut in half and sliced lengthways)
piece of fresh root ginger (3 cm long and 2 cm wide)
8 cloves garlic (peeled, crushed and chopped)
10 tbsp vegetable oil
10 cardamom pods (slightly crushed)
10 whole cloves
1 tsp whole cumin seeds
2 pieces cinnamon stick (4 cm long)
2 bay leaves

½ tsp ground turmeric
¼ tsp cayenne pepper
1½ tbsp ground, dry-roasted coriander seeds
½ tbsp ground, dry-roasted cumin seeds
3-4 tbsp natural yoghurt
1 large tomato (peeled and finely chopped)
1 tsp salt

Put the two chopped onions, with the peeled and chopped root ginger and the garlic, with 3 tablespoons of water into the bowl of a food processor and process to a smooth paste.

Blanch the cauliflower florets in boiling water until barely tender. Trim the ends from the aubergine and cut it into quarters lengthways. Chop each quarter into 2 cm pieces. Place the pieces of aubergine into a strainer and sprinkle all over with salt. Allow them to stand for 20 minutes. This removes much of the bitter flavour and some of the liquid from the vegetable. Rinse thoroughly under the tap and then pat dry the pieces with kitchen paper.

In a wide, heavy-bottomed frying-pan heat 8 tablespoons of oil and fry the sliced onions in this, over a medium heat, until they are dark brown in colour and crisp but not burnt. Remove the onions with a slotted spoon and place them to drain on kitchen paper. Add the remaining oil to the pan. Now add the cinnamon sticks, the bay leaves, the cardamom pods, the cloves and whole cumin seeds to the pan. Stir and fry for 1 minute before adding the paste from the food processor. Fry this, stirring constantly, for 10 minutes. Adjust the heat to prevent it burning. Add the dry-roasted ground coriander and cumin, the ground turmeric and the cayenne pepper. Fry and stir for 1 minute.

Stirring all the time, add the yoghurt a tablespoonful at

a time, the chopped tomato, the salt, and after a minute or so about 125 ml of water. Stir to mix through. Now add all the prepared vegetables and thoroughly coat them with the sauce. Turn up the heat and bring the sauce to the boil. At this stage, I usually tip the whole lot into a pot large enough to hold everything and let it cook, gently, for another 30 minutes. Stir it from time to time without breaking the vegetables. Serve in a very hot serving dish with the browned onions as a garnish.

Tomato and Onion Relish

Serves 6:

2 large tomatoes (diced small)
2 smallish onions (peeled and finely chopped)
1½ tsp salt
2 tbsp lemon juice
½ level tsp freshly ground black pepper
1 heaped tsp whole cumin seeds (dry-roasted then ground)
pinch cayenne pepper

Prepare the tomatoes and onions, mix them together, and place them in a serving dish. Dry-roast the cumin seeds and then grind them in a mortar. Sprinkle the salt, lemon juice, black pepper and cayenne over the tomato and onion mixture. Mix them together and then refrigerate for 30 minutes. Before serving, sprinkle the roast ground cumin over the top of the relish.

Cucumber Raita

Serves 6:

1 large cucumber (peeled and grated)
500 ml natural yoghurt

1 tsp salt
¼ level tsp freshly grated black pepper
pinch cayenne pepper
½ tsp whole cumin seeds (dry-roasted then ground)

Put the yoghurt into a serving dish and beat it with a fork until smooth. Add the cucumber, the salt, pepper, cayenne and the roasted ground cumin and mix them thoroughly with the yoghurt. Refrigerate for 30 minutes. Serve garnished with a sprinkling of paprika for colour.

Index of Recipes

THE SECRET ARMY

J. Bowyer Bell

The Secret Army is the definitive work on the IRA. It provides an absorbing account of a movement which has had a profound effect on the shaping of the modern Irish state. J. Bowyer Bell, a specialist in the problems of unconventional war, terrorism, risk analysis and crisis management, has been a research scholar at Harvard and MIT and at the Institute of War and Peace Studies, Columbia University. He is now President of the International Analysis Centre in New York. He has written more than a dozen books, including *Assassin! The Theory and Practice of Political Violence* and *The Gun in Politics: An Analysis of Irish Political Conflict 1916-1986.*

POOLBEG

Terrible Beauty

Diana Norman

Constance Markievicz was the most remarkable Irish woman of her generation. Renouncing her Protestant Ascendancy upbringing, she threw herself wholeheartedly into the struggle for independence which dominated Irish politics in the first two decades of this century. A dedicated feminist, she campaigned for equality and suffrage for women, viewing these aspirations as part of the nationalist issue. An ardent socialist, she was committed, alongside Connolly and Larkin, to the cause of Labour and the freedom of workers.

Imprisoned several times by the British authorities and sentenced to death for her part in the Easter Rising of 1916, Constance Markievicz went on to win election in 1918 as the first woman member of parliament, and then the world's first woman Minister of Labour in the first Dáil Éireann. Her courageous action and politial achievements earned her the respect and affection of ordinary Irish men and women.

Diana Norman has written a warm and sympathetic biography, in which her subject's personality is shaped by the threefold influences of resurgent nationalism, feminism and socialism. Believing her to have received less than her full due from previous biographers, Diana Norman here restores Constance Markievicz to a pre-eminent position not just in Irish history but in the history of women in the twentieth century.

POOLBEG